MY LIFE:

Growing Up Asian
in America

MY LIFE:

Growing Up Asian

in America

EDITED BY

CAPE, the Coalition of Asian

Pacifics in Entertainment

With an Introduction by **SuChin Pak**

Entertainment
B O O K S

NEW YORK LONDON TORONTO SYDNEY NEW DELHI

An Imprint of Simon & Schuster, Inc.
1230 Avenue of the Americas
New York, NY 10020

First MTV Books/Atria Books hardcover edition May 2022

ATRIA BOOKS and colophon are registered trademarks of Simon & Schuster, Inc.

For information about special discounts for bulk purchases, please contact Simon & Schuster
Special Sales at 1-866-506-1949 or business@simonandschuster.com

The Simon & Schuster Speakers Bureau can bring authors to your live event. For
more information or to book an event contact the Simon & Schuster Speakers Bureau
at 1-866-248-3049 or visit our website at www.simonspeakers.com.

Interior design by Kyoko Watanabe

Manufactured in the United States of America

1 3 5 7 9 10 8 6 4 2

Library of Congress Cataloging-in-Publication Data is available.

ISBN 978-1-9821-9535-9
ISBN 978-1-9821-9537-3 (ebook)

Contents

Introduction

There is a Korean word, *han*, that is essential to our identity. Like a lot of very culturally specific words, the definition is hard to pin down. But it is, in essence, an emotional state of being that is somewhere between deep sorrow, resentment, and anger. Many Koreans equate this emotional state to a fire that sometimes rages and sometimes quietly smolders. This internalized energy can be destructive, but at times it is from this fire that we can find the seeds of our courage. *Han* captures the complicated quality of where I am today in my understanding of courage, better so than the American idea, which is always the fighter, the first one into battle, or the leader of the protest. I find that version of courage to be limiting and self-defeating. By that definition, I am a coward, which I know is not true.

As I write this introduction during the summer of 2021, courage has been on my mind a lot because I've been afraid so much lately. The rise in anti-Asian hate crimes that began in 2020 has made me scared for the safety of my parents and of my kids. I keep going back to the images and videos of our elders and our women especially, who have been spit on, beaten, and threatened because they are considered foreign menaces. And yet, in all the years I have been in the media, I have never seen such a public outpouring of our courage. I have never seen people share the stories of our isolation and fear in such a vocal way. And it moved me to share my own pain, something that I never imagined doing. And in this outpouring, so many of us, myself included, have found a way into courage that is as complex as our sense of who we are as Asian Americans today.

When I was a teenager, courage basically meant never saying no. It meant never wanting to miss out on an opportunity and saying yes to things that felt bigger than my own small world. As a high school junior, I said yes to an offer to host a weekly teen show that aired on my local news channel, not knowing then that this would be the biggest turning point of my life. Being a TV journalist wasn't my dream just yet, because even though I was working on television, I never once thought that I could actually make a living as a journalist. TV reporters looked like Diane Sawyer and Barbara Walters, not sixteen-year-old Korean American girls with frizzy bobs and acne. Yes, I had Connie Chung to look up to, but there was this sense that America had its one Asian American anchor—the job had been filled. I figured I would ride this stroke of luck as far as it would take me, and then my regular plan of becoming a lawyer, like a good Asian daughter, would resume.

Right from the beginning, cameramen told me to "open my eyes" and "squint less." It was always embarrassing to hear, to have my insecurities about the way I looked—so different from what an American should look like—validated again and again by people I felt had the right to pass this kind of judgment. But if being successful on their show meant adjusting my appearance, I was willing to pay what felt like a small price. Like most Asian American women, I had a lot of training to appear less Asian and more white. I have memories of sitting with my glamorous Korean aunties, who regularly praised how fair my skin was and how beautiful I would be as soon as I could get my eyes done. I have a roll of film from a summer in Hawaii spent with my cousins when I was nine, where in every single shot I am raising my eyebrows as high as they will go, giving me a perpetual look of shock. But my eyes are, indeed, wider. Eventually, I experimented with tape to fold my lids into a rounder shape. I practiced facial exercises that would slim my jaw and open my eyes. I did everything I could to take the cameramen's "helpful" tips to heart and thanked everyone around me, all the time, for the absolute privilege of the opportunity.

I fell in love with reporting on that job and found a new reserve of courage, this one telling me to chase this dream, to have the courage to say that this is what I wanted for myself. And I convinced myself—and my parents—that I could have a career in journalism. Thankfully, that turned out to be mostly true. My hard work paid off, and in 2001 I landed a job at MTV as a news correspondent, which put me in front of millions of people. I tiptoed around that space, terrified of screwing things up and always feeling like I was holding someone else's lottery ticket. I found my place in that world by hiding my fear and smiling a lot. I became very adept at making people—even terrible ones—comfortable by using flattery and humor. When I encountered inequality or unfair treatment because I was a woman and/or Asian American, I doubled down on nice or made jokes to defuse the tension. When it was really bad, I remained in what I imagined was dignified silence. I had convinced myself that if I voiced my dissatisfaction or anger, I would be jeopardizing my career. This is the pact so many of us make to fit into a society dominated by white supremacy:

If we play by their rules, we get to stay. My strategies would work . . . until they didn't. And then, in those instances, I would crawl into bed and cry and be enraged and spiral into fear.

I felt like a coward all the time. If I could just be the traditional version of courageous—bold, straightforward, forthright—maybe the unbearable weight of unworthiness and shame I was carrying could be lifted. But I didn't have it in me; I didn't know how to be that kind of brave. I experienced deep shame whenever someone commented on how "chinky" my eyes were and I said nothing in response. Or when I pretended to take it as a compliment when someone commented on how beautiful all Asian women were. I had been fed a very convincing narrative that if I didn't, in that moment, confront the racism, that if I ignored the ubiquitous ways Asian women are fetishized all the time, *I* was to blame. That I had blown things out of proportion. That they hadn't meant it that way. That I was being overly sensitive.

A couple of years into my time at MTV, my feelings of unworthiness gave way to anger. I was angry all the time—I tried so damn hard to be good, to follow the rules, and none of it seemed to make a difference. Every day I was on air felt like an audition. And everything I did—my mannerisms, what I wore, how my hair was done—was scrutinized by the executives. I constantly felt like I was on borrowed time, that they would replace me the moment they found a better person to fill my seat.

I hated their version of me, as it rubbed so sharply against the truth of who I knew I *wanted* to be. But whose fault was that? I had been complicit, hadn't I? I had let them have so much control over who I was and how I behaved . . . and I didn't know how to be any different. All I knew was, I no longer had it in me to be apologetic, grateful, and polite anymore. But what could I do with this anger? I was afraid if I lost my job, my family would struggle financially and I'd be seen as a failure. I was afraid that I'd never get hired again by another network. I felt no power to change my circumstances, and just as defeating, there was still a big part of me that wanted their acceptance and approval.

I see now that the shame, anger, and fear I was dealing with at this stage in my life have transformed the way I define courage today. I started to ask myself, *What will happen if I stop complying? What will happen if I stop smiling and being nice?* It is terrifying to ask these questions, but it's courageous. The simple awareness that these questions burn inside of us is courageous. I want to acknowledge—no, shout!—that courage can look very different from the image on the poster. It can look like someone who is shaking, crying, and emotionally undone. When I was crying because things felt unjust, when I was shaking with anger but unable to speak because I was still afraid, these are the moments I've come into awareness of myself and my worth. Those uncomfortable feelings guide us to an understanding that we deserve more. It was when I *wasn't* angry or an emotional wreck that I felt the most disconnected to who I was. In that kind of compliance, I was giving up on myself, giving in to their version of who I should be.

When I think back to all the times I didn't speak up, all the times I let it slide, every time I had to hide or contour my face to make it more palatable for the cameras, I think about how, alongside the seeds of unworthiness, I was also planting the seeds of this awareness. That's what I nurture now. I let the most complicated emotions guide me to where the injustice is. For me, this is the most courageous work of all: dismantling and reconciling my former shame and guilt while also honoring them. Every now and then, I watch old footage of myself—smiling, holding in so much emotion but still projecting intelligence and compassion—and I no longer see a coward. I see someone who is using all that she knows to survive, who is bravely navigating a world that doesn't value her.

Today, I find the most courage in the spaces where we tell our stories. For so long, I was scared to talk about my experiences, but I have found so much healing in this sharing and in hearing about others' journeys. When I've gotten lost in the crush of sadness scrolling through images of violence against our women and elders, when I've had to tell my daughter that today terrible things have happened and I'm too sad to get out of bed, the words of our community have given me hope and strength. *My Life: Growing Up Asian in America* brings together thirty of those voices—novelists, poets, journalists, activists, illustrators, and thought leaders—to reflect on what it was like to come of age in the United States. The experience of being seen as less American. The truth behind the model minority myth and our proximity to whiteness. The pain that comes from always being minimized and erased. The wisdom and shortcomings of our elders. How we internalize being mocked, laughed at, and dismissed. The beauty in finding friends and partners who see us as we are. They write about so many things that I wish I had known, and I am forever grateful to have their stories as part of a new understanding of self and community.

As I read their words, I have to stop a lot. I have to take deep breaths, let myself sit and feel things that I have practiced so hard to numb. I feel seen in a way that is both validating and, at times, very overwhelming. For all those years, I carried the anxiety and trepidation alone. So many of us have had to navigate the world on our own without the connection that is here on these pages. And now, here we are, holding this burden together, which makes it feel lighter . . . and makes me feel stronger. I can't help but think about how bold and deeply courageous we all are. These are early days in our transformation, and as we reexamine what our stories hold—past and present—we guide each other through what we have never said out loud before.

Another central aspect of *han* as I was taught is a loss of identity and the deep sorrow that comes from this loss. For many years, I lived in this emotional space, wondering who I was and who I was supposed to be. I still lose my way all the time, trying to answer those questions. In the past, I let others answer them, but I'm at a place now where the answers are my own. I hope the stories in *My Life* help you see the courage that already exists inside of you and that you will nurture both the moments when you feel bold and those when you feel vulnerable. Let all these aspects of courage guide you to find your truest self.

SuChin Pak
September 2021

Patiently educating a clueless white person about race is draining. . . . It's like explaining to a person why you exist, or why you feel pain, or why your reality is distinct from their reality. Except it's even trickier than that. Because the person has all of Western history, politics, literature, and mass culture on their side, proving that you don't exist.

—CATHY PARK HONG

Time

by Teresa Hsiao

There was the time in kindergarten when a little boy eloquently greeted me with, "Ching chang ching chong choo."

There was the time in Pizza Hut when our waitress eyed my parents and asked, very slowly, "Do you . . . speeaaaak Eeeengliiish?"

There were the many times I've been asked, "Where are you from?" followed by, "No, where are you *really* from?" I guess I'm from Boston, but I'm *really* from Indiana, where I was born.

But that never seems to be the right answer.

There was the time a store clerk asked my mom, genuinely curious, "So, do you folk celebrate Christmas?" There was the time I was complimented for not having an accent. There was the time a neighbor whispered of me and my brother, "They're so well assimilated!" as if they had expected us to start karate-chopping fish heads at any moment. There was the time I got so mad at my parents for not wanting to buy Lunchables; I just wanted to fit in and show that we, too, ate such normal things as pizza crackers.

There was the time, a few glorious years in elementary school, when I had a best friend named Lisa, a Vietnamese girl in my class. There were *many* times when people mixed us up, even though she was a foot taller and we looked nothing alike. But we had rhyming names and we were Asian, so that was enough. I cried for days when she moved to California in seventh grade. But my mom managed to find the silver lining: Now that I was the only Asian left in the entire school, she didn't have to introduce herself at parent-teacher conferences anymore. Everyone knew she was Teresa's mom.

There was the time in high school when my friends all wanted to get blond streaks in their hair, so I got them too . . . except that my hair refused to take on the Kelly Clarkson skunk look that was very cool at the moment and instead decided just to go gray.

There was the time in college when a guy hit on me by asking, "So, what kind of Asian are you?"

There was the time post-college when I was on a plane to the Midwest, and a very friendly, kind-eyed blond woman next to me said, "I've never met an Oriental before!"

There was the time I went to see *The Hangover* with a big group of friends, and when Ken Jeong made his surprise nude appearance we all laughed and laughed, but then after, I wondered if we were laughing at him and if that was okay, and why it seemed like anytime I saw Asian people in movies or on TV, we always seemed to be the butt of the joke.

There was the time I got my first job writing jokes for TV, and even though I was a professional writer, I still got asked to walk on someone's back. There was the time when, on a writing staff of twenty white men and only two women, I listened to a colleague complain about how hard it is for white men to get jobs now. There were many times when one of the writers would pitch something offensive about minorities or women, and there were many times when I felt like I had to laugh so as not to get the dreaded, "It's just a joke, relax"—like *I* was the problem. There was the time I was discussing racism against Asian Americans and a colleague said, "Well, you chose to come here," as if anything bad that happened to us was our fault, or the fault of our immigrant parents or ancestors. Because, you know, we were asking for it.

And then there is the time.

The time that is spent processing each of these little indignities and microaggressions, some that were innocuous and some that were designed to be hurtful, to make it abundantly clear that *you're not one of us.* Time that is spent explaining our culture and customs to people who have mostly seen us represented as exotics, as jokey stereotypes. Time that is spent recognizing our own privilege and appreciating the past generations who had it way, way worse. Time that is spent realizing the responsibility we have to be allies to other minority communities, and also support those historically marginalized in our own. Time that is spent feeling guilty that I actually had it pretty easy . . . but understanding that doesn't preclude me from deserving to be heard, that my megaphone shouldn't be dependent on some kind of competition of suffering.

All this time and energy that could have been spent working or playing but is instead spent on protests and activism and essays on what it's like to be Asian in America.

But even though change is slow, I look to the gains we've made as Asian Americans. Our community is louder and more united than ever. There are more Asian faces represented on-screen in everything from hit movies to trashy reality shows. There are more Asian stories being told for us, by us. We are showing that we don't have to be the butt of the joke—we can tell the joke. We don't have to hide our accents and assimilate to a culture devoid of us; we are part of the definition of what it is to be *us*, to be Americans. We are proudly asserting ourselves in this new world, one that is more open and culturally sensitive, one that cares about representation and not just as a hashtag.

Even though the Asian diaspora is large, collectively we have so much power, and we can use that to spread love and joy and kindness. And maybe one day, future generations won't have stories of growing up *Asian* in America . . . just growing up in America.

Of course, there is still work to do.

But hey—there is time.

Listen Asshole

by Yellow Rage
(Michelle Myers and Catzie Vilayphonh)

Michelle's Verse

Listen Asshole—

Stop trying to guess what I am
Stop trying to tell me what I'm not
I was born in Seoul, which makes me Korean
These slightly slanted eyes ain't just for seeing

Bitch, I see right through you—
you "expert" on me with your fake Asian tattoo
you "expert" on me with your Tae Bo and kung fu

So what, you tried dim sum and then some on the menu
So what, you a fan of Lucy Liu

So what, you read *The Joy Luck Club* too —
that makes you an "expert" on how I should look?

FUCK YOU

What the fuck do you know about being Asian?

I'm about to put you in your place, son.
What do you know about napalm and Saigon?

About Hiroshima and Nagasaki?
About Gandhi?

What do you know about demilitarized zones and No Gun Ri?
About My Lai and the military?
What do you know about the Killing Fields?
And signs that wield — "No Chinese or dogs allowed"?

What do you know about Comfort Women and "Geisha Girls"?
About colonization all over the Asian world?

What do you know about the Great Wall?
I can school you on each and all —

MOTHERFUCKER, *I'm about to get raw* —

What do you know about "revolution"?
About Ho Chi Minh and Mao Zedong?

I know it was Gil Scott-Heron who said, "The revolution will not be
    televised,"
so my membership in the revolution will not be based on how
    slanted are my eyes

My eyes on the prize—fight with all my might
against motherfuckers who think I'm a white girl
—*Watch my finger unfurl*

You picked the wrong Asian woman to mess with
because my tongue is split—it is forked and steel tipped
and it will puncture and bleed you

And if you don't know
now you know, Asshole.

Catzie's Verse
Asshole, listen
Don't ask me what I'm
saying in my native tongue
you want to know so badly,

go learn it yourself
20 years it took me
to perfect the language
my mother and her mothers spoke
20 seconds it took you
to have the nerve to ask me
what my sisters and I spoke
about
If I said I wasn't talking to you
why don't you stop bothering me—
all up in my business!

How dare you step to me
invade my privacy
waste my time and ask if I'm
able to relay you
the contents
in my conversation
what nonsense
is this?
Do I look like your private translator?
Nosy motherfucker
you probably thought dialogue centered around you
and you just wanted to make sure

Is that because you're paranoid and insecure?
Or just jealous 'cause my tongue's got more . . . skills than yours?
Ohhhh
so you wanna learn to say,
"*I love you*" and "*Hello*"
Why you need to know?
You think of me as some Asian ho
ready to turn around at your calls of
"*Hey baby anyonghasayo, anyonghasayo*"
or
"*Nee how mah, I love you China doll*"

Please
Your bullshit doesn't impress me at all
because my words
were meant
to be mentioned in
meticulous and mellifluous manner
yet your
mispronouncing manhandling mouth
fucks it all up
my meanings misused for miscommunication
misconstrued to a
misinterpreted

misspoken

mistake

muthafucka, that makes me mad

So you better

have listened asshole

and listen well

Don't talk to me anymore

Don't fuck with me anymore

Because I am done talking to you.

When we wrote "Listen Asshole" in 2001, it was intended as a bold and unapologetic response to intrusive questions frequently directed at us as Asian American women. We wanted to confront and repel those forces, which attempt to deny us of our complexities and full humanity. The poem also seeks to defy the stereotypes that many people perpetuate about Asian Americans and calls out the systematic erasure of Asian American history and experiences. It has always been our hope that by shattering stereotypes of Asian American women as being passive, quiet, and weak, we would empower and inspire other Asian American women to be strong, proud, and resilient. In 2021, we partnered with Studio Revolt to produce a short film of the poem as a response to the escalation in anti-Asian violence that occurred during the coronavirus pandemic; the film can be viewed on Studio Revolt's YouTube channel.

—MICHELLE AND CATZIE, AUGUST 2021

Rishi's Night:

A One-Act Monologue Play

INSPIRED BY A TRUE STORY

by Moss Perricone

Setting
Orange County, CA. 2009.

Characters
Rishi (fourteen, Indian, talks fast and spits a lot, especially when he's talking about movies)

An empty stage. Rishi enters. He takes a beat to register the audience. Then he starts.

Okay. So. Anyway. For this to make sense, you have to know about the uniforms at my school. That's St. Catherine's Episcopal School in

Rancho. Also, you need to know that Orange County, where I live, just became sister cities with Braga, a Portuguese city. I think it's a city. It's a sister city, so I guess it has to be a city. But Orange County isn't a city, so I actually don't know.

Also, you need to know *Slumdog Millionaire* just won Best Picture.

Okay, so—the uniforms. St. Catherine's Episcopal School has three uniform options for boys.

1. Blue polo with blue shorts
2. Brown polo with brown shorts
3. Brown polo with brown pants

Here's the thing: the brown uniform is the same color as my skin. And not just in a general brown way. There's a Hispanic kid in sixth grade and he's brown, but not *this* shade of brown. It's exact. And that's a huge problem cuz if you see me from far away, I look naked.

I'm not making that up. At this point everyone at school is used to it and knows I wouldn't, like, come to school naked. But if there's a sub or a new kid, they always look at me weird. Or if my mom picks me up from school and has to run errands, then I get looks wherever we go. If someone's really looking, I tug on the uniform to show that it's cloth and not my skin. But then I worry they think I'm naked *and* have, like, weird elastic skin. That freaks me out cuz then they're probably like, "Oh, he has some condition where his skin is elastic, so he *has* to be naked." Then I imagine, when their kids are complaining, they point at me and say, "Be grateful. You could be naked and elastic like that boy."

• • •

You're thinking I should wear the blue uniform. But the blue only has shorts. I don't wear shorts.

So, here's what happened. There was going to be a party. Like, a rager. Some senior at Capo High was throwing it. I don't know him. I don't know any high schoolers. Anyway. This senior made a Facebook event for the party and I guess he, like, accidentally made the event public. So, it came up on my feed. He must've realized, cuz when I checked the next day it was gone. But I had already written down the address.

Wait, it weirds people out when I say I don't wear shorts. And I'm going to tell the story, but real quick. . . . I haven't worn shorts since fifth grade because that's when I started getting hair on my legs. And I know you're thinking that I'm ashamed of my hairy legs, but I'm not. I *was* when I first got the hair, cuz I was the first person in my grade to get it. It's scary to be the first person. For anything. Like, I was the first person in kindergarten to lose a baby tooth and I wedged it back in cuz I didn't want to be first. Then Brandon Davonport lost his and everyone thought that was *so* cool. I tried telling people I lost mine first, but no one believed me.

So, as soon as my mom was at work, I took her razor and shaved my legs. Great. Fine. But then, when the hair started to grow back, it was agony. It was all, like, pointy and sting-y. So, I started shaving my legs every night before they could get prickly. And that's why I don't wear shorts. Not because I have leg hair, but because I'm actually the only guy in eighth grade without it.

• • •

Anyway. Going to this party wasn't, like, simple. My mom's strict. And even if she wasn't, this was a high school party with alcohol and no parents where I didn't know anyone and wasn't invited. Like, obviously she wouldn't let me go. Plus, it was on a Thursday.

But I had a plan. I'd tell my mom I was going to a movie with my friend Lewis after school. Then I'd say Lewis invited me to spend the night. That way she wouldn't have to drop me anywhere and she'd have no opportunities to confirm with Lewis's mom. Of course, she might call Lewis's mom that night. So, the week before the party, I went to the movies with Lewis and spent the night for real to see what she would do. This was harder than it sounds cuz Lewis has bad taste in movies. But it went perfectly. My mom didn't check, and I convinced Lewis to see *The Reader*.

Of course, this whole plan had an obvious flaw. I'd have to show up to the party in my uniform. Which means that everyone would think I was:

    A. A middle schooler
    B. A middle schooler who wears their uniform all the time
    C. Naked

You might be thinking, *Just bring a change of clothes to school.* Okay, well, hold on. That's not easy. St. Catherine's has a zero-tolerance policy for uniform violations, so if I changed on campus, I'd get after-school detention. If I changed off campus, I'd have to carry a backpack all night. That's better than showing up in uniform, but not by much.

. . .

Anyway. I figured it out. If you walk from St. Catherine's to the Regal Cinema, you pass a bunch of trees. The day I went to the movies with Lewis, I filled an old backpack with party clothes, a box of condoms that I found on the street, and a cologne sampler from the mall. Then, on the walk to the movies, I flung the backpack up into a tree. On the day of the party, I'd leave school, retrieve the backpack, change, put my uniform in the backpack, fling it back into the tree, spend the night at the party, get my uniform, and head to school. Foolproof.

I was so excited. I couldn't sleep the night before. It felt like the night before *No Country for Old Men* and *There Will Be Blood* came to the UC Irvine theater on the same day. What a day.

At school, on the day of the party, somebody called me "Slumdog Millionaire." I don't remember who. I barely even noticed cuz I was so excited for the party. But it started happening a lot after that. And, like, I don't care. I really don't. I don't even know why I brought it up.

Anyway. I got out of school and—actually, wait. I didn't like getting called that. I still don't. I hate it, actually. Let me just tell you why.

1. *Slumdog Millionaire* premiered at Telluride in August. Everyone knows Telluride kicks off Oscar season. When a movie does well there, it's pretty much a lock for a Best Picture nomination.
2. It went to Toronto, where it won the People's Choice Award.
3. It swept the Writers Guild, Directors Guild, Producers Guild, and the Screen Actors Guild awards.

Nobody called me Slumdog Millionaire after any of that. They started, like, seven months later. Four days after it won Best Picture! How sad is that? A movie can win literally every award, but no one cares until it wins Best Picture. I mean, did anyone even see *Milk*? *Doubt*? *Waltz with Bashir*? I don't care when someone calls me Slumdog Millionaire, but when they don't start calling me that until months after it gets rave reviews at Telluride, wins Toronto, wins literally every critic and guild award, I despair for cinema. I really do.

I think that's why it bothers me.

And, like, it wasn't just "Slumdog Millionaire." It was "Slumdog," "Jamal," "that Indian guy from *Slumdog Millionaire*." That one was the worst cuz it's like, did you even see the movie? There are several Indian guys.

Anyway. I got out of school and went to get my backpack from the tree and . . . all of the trees were gone. They were gone. It was like there was never any trees. I just stood there. Trees don't just, like, go away.

I saw a landscaping crew. I asked them what happened. They were startled, I imagine, cuz they thought I was naked. One of them explained Orange County had just been gifted cherry blossom trees by their new sister city, Braga, and this is where they'd get planted. So, the other trees were cleared. I asked what they did with the things they found in the other trees. They asked what things. I wasn't going to say party clothes, condoms, and some cologne, so I changed my question. What happened to the other trees?

•   •   •

One of the landscapers explained the other trees had been auctioned off to pay for the cherry blossoms. That seemed messed up, because they were a gift. Who makes you pay for a gift? And, furthermore, who gives trees as a gift? That's a horrible gift. I was not loving the Portuguese in that moment.

The landscapers gave me the address where they had replanted the trees. It was in Coto. You know, the main gated community in Orange County.

The walk took three hours. It was mostly along highways. The house was massive. The trees were in the backyard. I knew cuz I could see the tops over the house. I just started walking along the side of the house. I held my breath for some reason.

Thankfully, there was nobody in the backyard. There was a pool with a rock grotto and a waterslide. There was a basketball court and a trampoline. The trees were clumped together like a little forest.

I started climbing the closest tree. I saw my bag on one of the branches. I felt relief—the bag could've been lost. I could've been trespassing for nothing. I took the bag and jumped. It was a long way down. It was so long that I had time in the air to:

1. Hear the back door open
2. Register it
3. Realize that I was screwed

Then I hit the ground. My knees buckled. I crouched there for a few seconds; then I remembered my realization from a moment ago: I was screwed. There was a man in the doorway looking at me. I wondered if I should run.

Then the weirdest thing happened. A boy around my age came out and asked the man what was wrong. The kid looked familiar. I didn't know him, but he looked familiar. The man said nothing was wrong. He thought he'd seen something in the tree. I swear, they were both looking *right* at me. Then they went inside.

I didn't move. I thought this was a trick. Then I realized what happened. I was standing against the tree. The trunk was brown. It was the same brown as my uniform, which, as you know, is the same brown as my skin. They didn't see me. They actually didn't see me! I'd accidentally camouflaged myself!

I sprinted all the way to the gate. As I ran, I imagined telling this story to the high schoolers. I imagined the whole party quieting down, leaning in, gasping at the reveal that I'd camouflaged myself. I replayed the whole thing in my head. Then I realized why the boy looked familiar. I stopped running. He looked familiar because he was wearing my clothes—my party clothes.

I opened my backpack. It was empty except for the box of condoms. Which was empty. I thought about going back. That's ridiculous. I couldn't, like, take the clothes off him. I didn't know what he'd done with the cologne or the condoms, but I figured I couldn't get those back either.

. . .

But look, here's the crazy thing. I still felt amazing. The whole thing gave me such a rush. Like, screw it. I'd go to the party in my uniform.

The party was in Lake Forest. Once I got within, like, a mile of the party, I could hear it. The street was covered in cars. They were blocking driveways. They were blocking the street. At the end of the cul-de-sac, I saw the party. The front door was open. I went in.

I realized immediately that it was so crowded that my body was blocked by other people's bodies, so no one could see my uniform anyways.

I saw a girl passing vodka. I positioned myself so I was the logical next person to pass to. She handed me the bottle. I'd never tried liquor. I took a sip and it felt fine in my mouth, but when I tried to swallow I almost spit it up. But I didn't.

Then "Ridin'" by Chamillionaire came on. Everyone sang along. Oh my god, it was so cool.

I saw somebody passing a paper cup and I got into position. Here's what I'd learned: the trick to parties is positioning yourself in rotations. I'd wasted so much time watching break-dancing tutorials on YouTube. No one was break-dancing.

I took a sip. This time, I spit it up. I spit it up on everyone. It was purple. I knew the taste. Robitussin. Everyone I spit on was yelling at me. Then everyone at the party was yelling at me. Everyone started to move. I realized two things:

1. They weren't yelling at me.
2. The police were here.

Everyone ran to the backyard and started jumping the fence. But that took me too long to figure out. I was behind. If I ran, I'd get caught. I thought about *National Geographic* and how lions always eat the slowest antelope. I was the slowest antelope. And then I noticed the walls. They were brown. They were the exact brown I needed. I wasn't the slowest antelope—I was a chameleon. A chameleon in, like, a herd of antelope. I was going to be okay.

I pressed myself against the wall and held still.

The cops saw me immediately. It didn't fool them at all. Like, not even a little bit.

They put me in the car and took me to the station.

My mom picked me up. I was basically grounded forever. It was a bummer. But, actually, it wasn't that much of a bummer. It was February, and everyone knows that's when the studios dump their worst movies.

Later that year, I took the PSAT. It was Saturday and there were high schoolers taking the SAT. I noticed a high schooler looking at me. He was with a group. They were all looking. I stretched my shirt to show that it was a shirt and not, like, my skin. He walked over. I prepared to fake laugh at whatever stupid thing he was going to say about *Slumdog Millionaire*.

. . .

He asked if I was at the party in February. I said yeah. The rest of the group introduced themselves. Apparently, everyone at Capo had been talking about some middle schooler who pressed himself against the wall to hold off the cops. It gave everyone time to escape. I almost told him that I wasn't trying to help anyone. I was actually trying to camouflage myself. But I decided to just take the credit. They said that everyone would be excited to have me at their school next year.

Anyway. That was pretty cool.

Blackout.

I Don't Want to Write Today

by Shing Yin Khor

I don't want to write today.

I don't want to write about violence today.

I don't want to write about honor or duty or respect today.

I don't want to write about the diaspora. I don't want to explain again to white people that I am Chinese, but I am Malaysian, and I do not dream of China.

I want to write about love.

I want to write about love, but I do not want to write about interracial love.

I don't want to write about the sacrifices of my parents.

I don't want to tell jokes about them — those are my jokes, not yours.

I don't want to write another food story. I don't want to draw another pair of chopsticks, I have drawn so many. Drawing chopsticks is easy. This is all easy if you know how to play the game.

I don't want to write about my family's rituals, or our prayers, or the distinction between culture and religion. I don't want to write about Chinese New Year, I don't want to write about cheng Meng, I don't want to write about hungry ghosts.

I don't want to write work taught to white students so they might understand me.

I don't want to tell white girls about the gods we worship or our funerals, or our temples.

They will take them.

They will write about universal grief writing about my grief. They will put my words in a white man's mouth.

They will win awards writing universal grief, but I will still be here, writing Chinese grief—only Chinese, never "universal."

I don't want to tell white people what my name means.

It is beautiful.

I will not write it in Chinese characters so they can look it up.

They do not deserve that knowledge.

I don't want to write work that is a must-read in May.

I don't want to write work that is a must-read when an auntie is beaten. I don't want to write work that is a must-read when an auntie is dead.

I want to be the center of the universe because I cried; I want these satellites to acknowledge my gravity.

I don't want to tell stories about my people, I want to tell stories about ME.

I want to write about leather jackets.

I look great in leather jackets.

I want to write about Beowulf.

Hwæt!

Lo!

So!

Bro!

I want to write about trains. I want to write about Canada Pacific 374, the first transcontinental passenger train in Vancouver, which gets a birthday party every year.

I want to write about caterpillars. I don't know anything about caterpillars really, but white people write about things they don't know all the time.

I want to write mean replies to the white women who are going to assure me that of course I can write anything.

I want to tell them that yes, of course I can write anything.

Oh, but they meant well. I want to write like I *meant well*.

I want to be petulant and possessive and selfish.

I want to be gross and demanding, just like this.

I do not want to give you my stories, and I do not want to write today.

When people see us as heroes, they're forced to see us as humans.

—JEFF YANG

Destiny Manifest

by H'Rina DeTroy

When I was jabbing the return key to make my beetle-shaped wagon scurry along and not capsize in the Kansas River, the computer teacher handed each student a sheet of lined white paper. She told us to write a letter telling our fictional relatives that we had arrived at the end of the Oregon Trail and to describe what happened along our journey.

"Use your imagination," she said.

My twelve-year-old self usually didn't mind writing. But it was early in the morning and a frigid spring day. I was tired and moody. *Dear Family,* I wrote in pencil. *We have arrived.* My mind went blank. My hand scribbled a few more words, attempting to put something else down. *I hate the fucking Oregon Trail and I hope you die.*

I reread those words, and I felt the thrill of uttering something powerful—followed by fear. The bell rang, and instead of handing the paper to the computer teacher, I folded it and hid it beneath the keyboard and left, my stomach fluttering.

This was sixth grade, by which time I had decided I *hated* playing *The Oregon Trail*. It was corny not only for being an age-appropriate computer game foisted upon us as an educational tool, but also for its rudimentary pixelated images in an era when Sega Genesis had already outpaced Nintendo in eye-popping graphics.

But I had also somehow become the kid who resented the school version of American history with its yearly displays of sawdust dioramas of colonial log cabins and fences made from Popsicle sticks. A question had started to creep into my mind: Why did school present only the side of history where almost all the important figures were white and male? I couldn't help but wonder if other people and perspectives were being left out. If it was historically accurate in *Oregon Trail* to say that some westward settlers experienced "Indian attacks," then it would be also historically accurate to show how many Native Americans perceived the caravans of countless covered wagons as an invasion. How could you reduce an entire group—a nation of people—to side characters or merely obstacles to get around? To me, the use of the *Oregon Trail* computer game sent a clear message that school and the people who controlled school were content designating one version of events as the official story, rubber-stamping it as History—even if it erased an entire people.

I was a half-Montagnard, half-white kid with a budding racial consciousness that was fed and high-octane fueled by television, and especially MTV. Late 1980s and early 1990s Black sitcoms, pop music, hip-hop, and fashion addressed race and racism directly, inspiring images of a multiracial, global utopia. Even if it was a few years after the album's release, I felt secretly that I was a foot soldier of Janet Jackson's Rhythm Nation and that when people were erased, ignored, or experienced discrimination, it was my fight.

I was called into the principal's office later that day. As I sat in his office, again my stomach fluttered because I had been caught. The principal was a kind, old, white man. He asked me about the letter. I told him I didn't mean it. He said that it was okay and that I was probably going through a lot. I said I was fine even though I was going through something. But I was young and didn't know how to name what it was. While I lacked understanding of what it meant to be Montagnard—to have indigenous, ethnic minority Vietnamese heritage—I did understand what it felt like to be unseen in books and movies and on television. There hadn't been a well-defined Asian American community where I had been raised, and a 1968 issue of *National Geographic* was the single reference I had for who my mother's people were.

I also lacked the language to describe the jumble of thoughts and emotions gripping me at the time. I was the new kid, having just moved from my mother's house in Connecticut to live with my white father in Maine. Deep down, I suspected myself of discrimination and treating my mother unjustly—a thing that filled me with shame. I devalued her because she couldn't wield English, her third language, as well as my white friends' parents. I'd watch her fumble to understand social and cultural cues and do anything to separate myself, as if I could erase her. My mother would never belong. *I hate the fucking Oregon Trail and I hope you die* was the language I had, gesturing clumsily at the anger, sorrow, isolation, and guilt I felt crisscrossing inside me. A world that unquestionably accepted simplified stories like *Oregon Trail* would never be one in which me, my mother, and our complicated relationship would ever make sense or belong.

Perhaps it's ironic, then, that years later I'd find myself and the language to parse the feelings of un/belonging at college in Eugene, not far from the Oregon Trail's destination. The influence of a relatively large and politically active Asian American student body made me believe I was allowed to claim my Montagnard heritage. I took an Asian American literature course where in scenes or stanzas, dialogue or dramatic works, I found the rift with my mother mirrored back to me through characters real or created. Hovering above these pages, I had enough distance to see how a relationship strained by generational differences was further challenged by language difficulties, cultural clashes, discrimination—and internalized racism. We weren't alone, my mother and I. Generations of authors and artists had named this pain, weaving multilayered narratives representing the lives and communities also deserving to be included and rubber-stamped as History.

These days, "Montagnard American writer" and "teacher" are identities I claim. I'm lucky to have had a chance to build inventive ways for others in the Montagnard diaspora to engage with history— and our erasure from it. Working with a community-based refugee organization in North Carolina, I created and taught Apocalypse Never: Writing Our Origin Stories and Imaginative Futures as Montagnard Americans, the first writing workshop to center our experiences and identities. Pushing boundaries further, we interrogated whether Asian American movements sufficiently included brown Asians and Pacific Islanders. I'd learn that our story wasn't so different from that of Native Americans, and that the settler-colonizers in our ancestral land were the ethnic Viet Kinh who, in designating us as "primitive," had also voided us from history. The participants taught me things about our heritage that I doubt were discussed or shared in any American classroom. Together, we created space to voice the myriad emotions accompanying a tangled history—the knots of our love and pain that defied simple, one-sided stories about ourselves, our families, and community.

For one exercise, I led workshop participants to develop fictional characters and set them in a specific time and place of our not-too-distant past. *Write a scene from the point of view of a Montagnard child, adult, or elder during the late 1950s in Vietnam when we demanded land rights, political participation, and the preservation of tribal languages in schools.*

"Use your imagination," I tell them—that creative pulse to help us radically re(en)vision our past, forge new paths, and manifest what comes next.

Going Country

by Nathan Ramos-Park

I grew up near cornfields, catching crayfish in shallow creeks, apple picking for hot cider during the changing seasons, stealing off at twilight to kiss boys to the sounds of bullfrogs and cricket symphonies. My life was like an idyllic coming-of-age film, until it wasn't.

My father, the first of his Filipino family born in America, was stationed in Korea during military service; my mother was a Korean pig farmer. My dad met my mom, and the two of them settled down in small-town Ohio. I didn't know I was different, being a mixed Asian extrovert (read: gay), but I could sense it. My kindergarten teacher narrowing her eyes, pretending I got answers wrong. My first-grade teacher putting me in the lowest reading level even though I already read chapter books.

Despite the damage, I grew up loving the idea of Americana—a barefoot kid who ventured out into the world when the sun came up and made it home in time for dinner. Being a young queer youth, I loved everything that was forbidden: dancing, fashion, art, singing.

Of all the musicians from my childhood, country superstar Faith Hill was my favorite. The first time I heard her voice, my mind blossomed like a sycamore tree. Faith Hill was an impossibly beautiful blonde with sun-kissed skin, perfect white teeth, and god-fearing curves, singing about what it meant to be in love. She was perfection to me. And she planted the tiniest kernel of a dream, a shameful desire in my heart: to be a country singer.

I was deeply in love with country music; I couldn't consume it fast enough. It was an entire world of storytelling: cheating husbands and vindicated wives, open roads and blue skies, first love and heartbreak. The first song I ever sang for an audience was "Desperado" by the Eagles—a gangly gaysian in dirty denim, crooning to an auditorium of rapt white faces.

When I was nineteen, I made it to the finals of Ohio Idol, a local collegiate singing competition akin to *American Idol*. To advance through the rounds involved a combination of judges' scores and audience support. The contestants were made up of pageant girls in beautiful dresses, clean-cut boys with gelled-back coifs, and me, with my spiky hair and a pastel tie. I was shocked at my own progress, and by the looks of others, they were too. An Asian boy in the Midwest who could sing? Was I just a novelty?

The night before we performed, a woman messaged me: "You don't NEED this. There are people here with REAL dreams that could ACTUALLY make it that NEED this win." It was a coded message. I couldn't tell explicitly that it was about race, but growing up in Ohio, I was allowed to be a part of something, but it always had its limits. I was allowed to be good at piano until it became "Of course the Asian kid is good at piano." I could do well in school until "Of course the Asian kid got an A." It's astounding how many ways someone can tell you to "go back to your country" even though you grew up next door.

As the rounds progressed, I realized that there was a good chance I could win the competition. But to this woman, who wasn't even competing, I was a threat. Even though I was singing classic American songs, I wasn't her vision of what an Idol should look like. She couldn't extend her aspirations to my personhood. I thought that would be the last negative message, that if I won the competition I could prove her wrong. I had spent my entire life in Ohio. I was deserving of being its Idol.

And its Idol I became. I received the highest marks in both judges' score and audience vote. I was crowned Ohio Idol. I had thought that woman's message would be the last piece of hate mail I'd get, but outside the auditorium the floodgates opened. Accusations of cheating, numerous death threats. The malignant racist undertones and overtones were relentless. I had intense anxiety going out in public, let alone to a party or class. The glares from strangers, vicious confrontations from friends of contestants, and hostile silence from the local singing community told me that everyone wanted me gone, not just from the party, but from the planet. I was not the Idol Ohio wanted. The one thing I loved was bringing me so much pain, so I quit all musical engagements and shelved my dream of being a country singer.

I found myself years later, now an award-winning playwright, on my first professional writing assignment for a digital sketch comedy show that I also starred in. We were asked to think of a comedy musical number, and I excitedly pitched a country song about being a gay Asian. It was crickets from the room full of straight white faces. We had sketches about alien dating apps and demonically possessed coworkers, but the idea of a gay Asian man singing country was a step too far. I remember the hesitancy, the asking for clarity. And the "let's put that idea on the back burner." But instead of shrinking myself, instead of accepting that choice, I went home that night and wrote a song. I poured my love of country music, of being queer, and of being Asian into the music. And the next day, with guitar in hand, I sang the music I loved for the first time in ten years. The joy came flooding back, as did the croon and crack in my voice. And this time, instead of singing a white singer's lyrics, I sang about my own experience. The song was greenlit and, a few months later, was nominated for a Queerty. (I lost to Trixie Mattel—an iconic defeat.)

This was the first time I found clarity through resistance. That by speaking up, I could make space for myself. Using my voice became this radical form of self-love. I was so used to apologizing for my existence and relinquishing control. And I had been taught my entire life not to advocate for myself. As long as I kept my head down and my feet moving, I'd get to my destination. But that, in fact, isn't true in America. I continually found myself at the gates with the entrance barricaded. It was time to open them by any means necessary.

Two years later, I worked on *Club Mickey Mouse*, a revamp of the *Mickey Mouse Club*, the origin story for so many (white) stars: Britney Spears, Justin Timberlake, Ryan Gosling. It was the most American of experiences—the making of stars using Disney Magic. This time around, we wanted the cast to actually reflect today's youth, so we searched from a wide swath of backgrounds. Inadvertently, four of the eight Mouseketeers identified as Asian American. Their parents had nurtured their love of singing and dancing, a far cry from my upbringing. I was astounded by their talent and speechless from their swagger (my age never more evident, using the word "swagger"). They taught me about how some songs were "bops" before "bops" entered popular lexicon, and as a millennial, I felt solidly in the Gen Z "know." But a part of me felt a tinge of resentment. I wished so badly to experience the world the way they did.

One day, the youngest Mouseketeer hit a mental roadblock. She was having trouble singing a passage of a song; her voice kept catching in her throat. Her eyes began to mist. I took her aside, and she told me how she was terrified of letting "us" down. That there had never been more than one Asian Mouseketeer and it was scary to be representing so many people for the first time. I immediately felt shame for how I had felt—even though these kids had chances I never had, they still carried the weight of representing our whole community. The burden of the Asian American experience rested heavily on her shoulders.

For so long, I felt like I was on an island, like I didn't have a community. It always felt like me against an endless horde, that I would be fighting alone forever. But in that moment, I realized she was right there along with me, toeing the line, braving the crashing waves of expectation. I held her hand. We took a deep breath together. For the first time, I wasn't the scared kid being shunned, but the mentor. And I told her what I wished I could have told myself all those years ago, standing on the Ohio Idol stage: "Today, you are doing your best. That is all you can do. Tomorrow might be better, it might be worse, but all we can do is our best. Anyone who criticizes you—that's a reflection of their fear, not your talent." She got back in the booth and finished the session. And thank god for Auto-Tune.

I had an epiphany shortly after that interaction. This young Mouseketeer was standing on my shoulders, looking to the future. And she already felt the next generation climbing atop hers to get closer to the mountaintop. All of us were just hoping for a glimpse of the endless expanse of possibility. Our community has so many dreams, and in order to achieve them all, we can't do it alone. The system keeps telling us there can only be one of us who can succeed, only to inevitably be swallowed up by a sea of white faces. That is a myth. We *can* create generational prosperity, infrastructure, and, most importantly, cultural change.

Faith Hill's biggest hit, "Breathe," starts: "I can feel the magic floating in the air. Being with you makes me feel that way." I feel that every time I'm around my Asian American kin. Asian American identity constantly grows and changes; already, these Mouseketeers' life experiences were light-years ahead of my own. But we were still inextricably bonded. I've learned it's not about the purity of who we are, but about the diversity of the diaspora. Each experience adds to the accumulation of our collective conscience. Because of others who came before me, I grew from a scared kid singing alone in his bedroom, to someone asking to be seen, to a creative professional now making space for our newest voices. Let's keep spreading that magic.

Confessions of a Banana

by Heather Jeng Bladt

If you ever want to see the real you, look at a picture of the back of your head. Go ahead. Take a selfie, but from behind. Did you discover a bald spot forming? Gray hairs you never knew existed? A misshapen head? Frizzy or wayward locks that you were too busy to take the time to style correctly? I recently came across said picture by accident and was sent into a total spiral. *Whoa! When did I get so blond? Should I dye it back to black? Definitely not, that'd be too scary. But is* this *what I want people thinking of me?*

I've been highlighting my hair blond since I was a junior in high school and my mom finally succumbed to my cute-but-not-so-cute begging. We had come to a compromise: I wouldn't dye it all blond, just highlights, thus preserving some of my boring, straight, black Chinese hair. Since then, I have endured more than two decades of bleach, of roots endlessly growing out, the extra cost of shampoo and conditioner for color-treated hair, and countless hours of falling asleep while sitting in salon dryer chairs (they're so toasty!), all so I can live by a notion I picked up at a very young age: you must hide who you are to fit in with those around you.

Have you ever heard the little ditty kids sing on the playground that goes: "I went to a Chinese restaurant to buy a loaf of bread. They asked me what my name was, and this is what I said: '*L-i-l-i*, chickaly, chickaly, pom-pom beauty, don't drink whiskey, Chinese, Japanese, Indian chief. Good grief!'"? It's accompanied by kids pulling their eyes in different directions to mock those ethnicities. On a blistering hot Yorba Linda, California, day when I was in the first grade, a little white boy came up to me on the playground and interrupted my sweaty game of tetherball to sing me this song. I turned bright red and froze in a panic as I looked around at all the other kids laughing at me. For the first time in my life, I realized I was not like most of the others in my predominantly white school. I wanted to run away and cry, but in the (literal) heat of the moment, I made a different choice: I sang the song back to him, pulling my eyes every which way.

And it killed.

Because of that success, of being the Asian who laughs at the racist jokes instead of the Asian you make fun of, I decided to maintain the reputation to ensure my safety. To my great shame, I made fun of the other few Asian kids at school and I refused to play with them. I stopped eating white rice, fried rice, rice of any kind. When my parents told me stories about my ancestors, I tuned out, uninterested in my big Chinese family, how we got here, and how I came to be. I did everything I could to shun my Chinese heritage. I became racist against my own people. Racist against myself.

There are plenty of things not to like about oneself growing up, but to hate one's heritage? That's rough. It meant I didn't respect my parents and ancestors on some level. And the primary Chinese lesson that had actually survived the three generations we had been in the United States was to respect one's elders. I felt guilty for being ashamed of the people who loved me for being me, but I still spat in the face of their love because I wanted to fit in with the rest of the world so desperately. All because I did not want to have another racist song sung at me. And because of something so trivial, I pressed on with trying to hide the Chinese in me, very much in the same way I tried to hide the fact that I had believed in Santa Claus until I was *thirteen years old*. Both were embarrassments that I hoped no one would uncover. Yet, unlike my belief in Santa Claus, being Chinese wasn't exactly easy to hide. Still, I tried. I studied how to be white, which wasn't hard, considering most movies and TV shows at the time had all-white casts. I repeated catch-phrases from *Full House*, permed my hair so I could have curls like Topanga from *Boy Meets World*, and got fashion tips from the cast of *Dawson's Creek*. But even though I walked the white walk and talked the white talk, I sure as hell wasn't white.

This became glaringly apparent to me when my hormones (the enemy of us all) kicked in and I started to like boys. Since I had conditioned myself to revere all things white, it will come as no surprise that I crushed hard on the white boys. The feeling was not mutual. Pretty soon, I found myself in a real-life romantic comedy, but instead of being the lead, I was playing the role of the quirky, dumpy, and frenzied best friend. I helped my white girlfriends with their boy problems but never had a boyfriend of my own. White guys had no interest in me romantically, and it made me feel like I wasn't white enough or, rather, *good* enough for them.

Due to my infatuation with all things white, I had also conditioned myself to find Asian boys unattractive. Which, I knew, even at the time, was horrible. I love my dad and had never thought of him as unattractive. He's the charmer who won my mom's heart, after all. But Asian boys didn't have any allure for me. However, I was so desperate for a boyfriend—definitely a symptom of all the (white) princess movies and romantic comedies I had studied—that I didn't care which boy liked me. If the white boys didn't like me, maybe the Asian boys would? That's when I decided to let the Chinese in me shine through for the first time in a long time . . . all because I wanted a boy to like me.

At this point, I was very comfortable being the only Asian in a crowd of white people. I knew how to talk about their interests; I pretended my family had the same values as theirs; I rolled with their racist punches. But crossing the cafeteria to the Asian table to look for love was totally out of my comfort zone. As I made the interminable lonely walk over to a group of people who looked like me, I could feel their eyes seeing right through me as I approached—they knew I was not one of them. Still, I sat down and awkwardly tried to make conversation. They weren't having it. They proceeded to probe me with questions, trying to figure me out.

They asked me if I spoke Chinese.

"No, I don't."

They asked me if my parents spoke Mandarin or Cantonese.

"Um, they don't speak Chinese either. But my grandparents do! I mean, a little bit."

They asked me which dialect my grandparents spoke.

"Oh, uh . . . I'm not sure."

They kept trying to fit me into some Asian box that they understood, but with each question came an answer that disappointed them. It confused them that I didn't know what city my ancestors were from. And with each question, I became more confused myself.

The part of me I had been trying to hide for so long wasn't even that Chinese. So, what had I been hiding this whole time? What was I? *Who* was I?

My Asian American classmates deemed me a "banana" because I was yellow on the outside and white on the inside. This felt like an insult because they were saying I wasn't enough of anything to belong to a group. I was all kinds of mixed-up . . . and they weren't wrong. However, even if I had embraced my Chinese heritage when I was younger, it wouldn't have mattered to them or my search. I still wouldn't have spoken Chinese or known how to be Chinese because of the fact that I'm third generation.

Many of my Asian American classmates were immigrants or the children of immigrants. But my great-grandparents were the ones who had left the motherland in the early 1900s to immigrate to the United States. My grandmothers were born here, my parents were born here, and thus the groundwork was laid for me to be born here. However, even before all this, my great-great-great-grandfather and my great-great-grandfather had come to the United States to work, but they had moved back to China after their sons took their places in America. When my ancestors immigrated here, there was a lot of anti-Chinese sentiment because white men were mad that the Chinese were taking all the low-paying jobs. This gave birth to America's first anti-immigration laws in the form of the Chinese Exclusion Act of 1882. The only way to survive was to assimilate to the Western ways. They stopped speaking Chinese. They adopted Western attire and religion. They did what they could to keep the fact that they were Chinese hidden. Sound familiar?

I wasn't white enough, but I wasn't Asian enough either. I discerned that I would not be accepted for being somewhere in between.

So, I did what my ancestors before me did—I became chameleonlike, letting others project what they wanted to see onto me. I kept my head down and my mouth shut and allowed people to speak for me. It was then that I lost all sense of who I was.

For years, I stuck to this plan. Academically, I excelled in school. Since my classmates and teachers saw me as Asian, they assumed I was headed for a career as a doctor, and not wanting to disappoint anyone, I did too. However, during a high-school career day, I was bored by the doctor I had chosen to hear speak, so I wandered out of the classroom and into another where a screenwriter was presenting. My brain exploded. *You can write movies and TV? And get paid to do it?* I had always liked writing because I could craft stories about the people I longed to be. And now this woman was telling me I could write for the media I had learned so much from. The media that allowed me to escape from being me.

For the first time in a long time, I did something that called attention to myself: I raised my hand. I needed to know the path to take to become a screenwriter badly enough to risk getting made fun of. Thankfully, this woman gently explained her screenwriting journey to me and how it all started when she got into the four-year undergraduate screenwriting program at the University of Southern California. She mentioned that not many are accepted to the program, but I was undeterred. After school, I immediately went to the library to find what I needed to do to apply.

CUT TO:

My first day of my first screenwriting class at the University of Southern California. I had been accepted! And I was so excited to be sitting in buildings named after the filmmakers of *E.T.* and *Back to the Future*. I was ready to tell the stories of those I observed around me (it truly didn't cross my mind to tell my own stories). But the first topic on deck was "finding your voice." My voice? Who wants to hear *my* voice? According to my professor, that's what audiences want to see and hear—that's what makes great stories.

All my mixed-up feelings bubbled back up to the surface. Who am I? What am I? What do I have to say? I was sent into a panic. I'd spent the formative years of my life being whatever others wanted me to be. But the truth was I didn't know who I was; I had no idea how to write in my own voice. What I did know was: I'm not Asian enough. I'm not Chinese enough. I'm not white enough. I'm not smart enough. I'm not a good enough writer. I'm not a good enough daughter. I'm not a good enough sister. I'm not "anything" enough to be able to speak with authority about anything at all.

I took a deep breath—I'd just gotten to college, and I wasn't about to give up on the first day. I gave the assignment a lot of thought. By telling me to find my voice, my professor was asking me to be me. She was telling me that my stories had value . . . telling me that I was good enough. No one had told me that before.

I had come to an impasse. If I wanted to succeed as a screenwriter, I couldn't hide anymore. So, I dipped my toe in, at first writing quirky but innocuous stories about myself. After I received warm receptions to these personal stories, I found I didn't want to hide anymore. I began writing increasingly personal stories, where I was the star, not the quirky best friend. And over the course of four years, I found my voice. The whole college experience allowed me to become more comfortable with who I was.

After graduation, I wanted to tell a story about growing up in my parents' short-lived Chinese restaurant. I had a script and pitch ready to go for a pitchfest. But when I sat down at the table across from two execs drinking overpriced bottles of water, I was met with blanket statements that audiences didn't want to watch movies or TV shows about Asians, especially not with females in the lead. I tried not to let this get me down, but the other execs I pitched to had similar feedback. I wanted to make it as a screenwriter, so I slipped back into my old ways and wrote scripts with white male leads. It's hard to go against that survivor's instinct, to do whatever is necessary to blend in. To turn a blind eye to what so many generations before me have instilled in me: don't call attention to yourself, don't cause problems, be what everyone else wants you to be because their happiness will be how you succeed. Who am I to go against the system?

I spun out with this question for a while. Years actually. I'm a little dense. Remember the aforementioned too-long belief in Santa Claus? That lasted till I was thirteen. This lasted till I was thirty-three. During those spinout years, I kept to the status quo by writing other people's stories. It wasn't getting me gigs. So, while I was working as an assistant to movie and TV producers and writers, I experimented, writing myself and my family into my scripts, but assigning their race as white. People seemed to respond to this well, even though something still felt false to me.

In these years, I married my husband, Christian, who is a mix of Danish, German, English, and maybe some French. And then we had our *hapa* (half-Asian, half-white) son, Felix. Because I had come to respect the Chinese in me, a weird thing occurred when Felix was born: I couldn't help but be disappointed that he didn't look like me. He looks a lot like Christian—very white. This sent me into a spiral of guilt. I had already decided for this baby that he was going to hide his Chinese heritage. What had I done? I was letting my ancestors down; they would now not live through the next generation. I had successfully hidden the Chinese forever. I wanted to take it back. I had horrible thoughts about whether or not I should have married a white man. I questioned my relationship and how true the love was if I had fetishized all things white. I wanted my kid to be Chinese! And I wanted him to look Chinese because it's the only way I knew how to be. But the fact of the matter was, my son was half-white. Did I not love that part of him too?

And then I turned thirty-three. Trump had been elected. Anti-immigrant fervor exploded, giving rise to immigrant voices. I heard their stories and realized that they were just like my ancestors'. If they weren't let in, generations of children like me would never exist. The lightbulb turned on. I had found my answer. I realized I didn't have to go with or against the system my ancestors had put in place; there was a third option. I'm neither white nor Chinese. I'm American. And being American means that I can be whatever I want to be. I understand now that my ancestors hid for so long because they couldn't be themselves at that time. The same is not true for me. My generation is being asked to step into the light. To give voice to those who were silenced for so long. It's my duty to tell the stories that were lost along the way—to live the life they could not have. It's a lot of pressure, but it's time to change. It's actually imperative, because now I have two kids, Felix and my daughter, Lucy. I don't ever want them hiding anything the way I, and those before me, had to. I want them to be proud of all parts of who they are and where they come from. They are more than good enough. They are worthy. And from them, I'm slowly learning I'm worthy too.

Change is not easy and never happens overnight like I want it to.

I never magically wake up twenty pounds lighter, and Marie Kondo never sneaks into my house while I'm sleeping. It's a struggle to remember I don't have to hide anymore, after all those years of pretending. But it feels good when I get to say my truths. I'm still learning about the world and my place in it, which makes this a day-by-day process. But today, I'm looking at that picture of the back of my head again: streaks of long black and blond hair cascading into each other, winning the battle (for now) over the grays. Blond is no longer my way of trying to hide myself; black is no longer my shame. They both represent me and my past, like a badge of honor. My hair is a symbol of two worlds that have become one. I stand taller. Prouder. A smile creeps over my face. This is me.

Bangla, in Black and White

by Tanaïs

In a St. Louis library in 1990, I watched our people—speaking our language, eating with their hands—on an American big screen for the first time, in Satyajit Ray's iconic black-and-white film, *Pather Panchali*. This is the first film in his Apu Trilogy, a bildungsroman of the lives and tragedies of a young man named Apu. There was never any question of whether we, as Bangladeshi Muslims, saw ourselves in these Hindu characters living in rural West Bengal—they were our people too. Whereas books, the form I felt most drawn to, let my imagination run wild, I revered the emotional textures of this film. You cannot look away, neither from the suffering nor the joy. I wept when his sister, Durga, died from a fever, after dancing in the monsoon rains. I wept in the next two films, when Apu loses his mother, and his wife. The beauty of the trilogy imprinted itself on me as an artist, but so did the realization that feminine joy is short-lived in Satyajit Ray's films.

In 2021, I revisited Ray's prolific oeuvre. First up: *Charulata*, a story about a young *bhadramahila*, an upper-caste gentlewoman, set in late-nineteenth-century Bengal. It felt so relevant to me as I wrote a book, locked inside my home during quarantine, which made the character Charulata's plight intensely relevant. Stuck in the inner quarters of a palatial home, the *zenana*, Charulata passes time by playing card games with her sister-in-law, whom she can't stand, embroidering slippers, devouring books, and fixing tea for her husband, a man much older than she is. Too preoccupied with his newspaper and the rising freedom struggle against the British to pay her close enough attention, her husband arranges for his cousin, Amal the Poet, to come stay with them to keep her company. He's much closer to Charulata's age. This is where the delicious trouble begins. Besides living for free in a mansion, the Poet's task is to encourage her writing—even though Charulata is already a far better writer than he is—and each day that passes, her repressed sexuality is awakened.

(O, the eons of pedophiles arranged-married to child wives lost to younger men!)

• ⫶ •

In one of the most hypnotic moments in the film, Charulata rocks on a tree swing, breathes heavy, stares at the sky, mad—as in angry—with desire. From the angle of the camera, Ray makes sure we are close to her face, her breath, the rocking; we feel how much she wants to be fucked by this young man—how much she hates herself for this unshakable longing. With no way to expel their lust, the sweet, simple foreplay between herself and the Poet is a song, one that I recognized immediately. "Phule Phule Dhole Dhole"—"Flowers sway in the breeze." This was the first Bengali song I learned from my father. I remember Baj in his swimming shorts, transitioning my sister and me from baths to showers. I had no idea then that this song belonged to this film; when I sang it, I felt as though I was in my own world, unaware and unafraid of midwestern neighbors who hated our religion, our brown skin pearled and wrinkled by the falling water, our music, crystalline, bouncing off the walls.

. . .

Charulata writes a brilliant piece about her village for a paper that the Poet is too afraid to pitch to himself, and he realizes that she's way out of his league. When she falls into his arms, crying, "I'll never write anything again!," he also realizes that she's in love with him. Her tears flow, from the confusion, the guilt of writing him into oblivion, from knowing she'll never have him. Maybe the Poet is in love with her too. But he can never love her back—he would lose everything. And so, he leaves her, in the middle of the night.

(O, the husband is hotter than Amal, a fuccboi, but who can resist a Poet?)

. . .

Charulata is based on a novella, *The Broken Nest*, written in 1901, by the first Indian Bengali Nobel Laureate in Literature, Rabindranath Tagore, who also penned the lyrics to her song. Some say that the Poet's closeness to Charulata mirrored Tagore's real-life relationship to his sister-in-law Kadambari Devi. She was his elder brother's ten-year-old child-wife. In her husband's long absences from home, her bond with young Rabi, her peer, grew stronger. Did the two of them steal time away from the house? Or perhaps, on a rare afternoon, when they had the house to themselves, did they ever experience their forbidden love? When it came time for Rabindranath to marry, he, too, chose to wed a ten-year-old child, Mrinalini, whose father worked on his family's estate.

Four months later, Kadambari Devi overdosed on opium. Was death easier to face than losing the love of her life whom she'd never have?

. . .

A moment comes and goes in the film, nearly imperceptible:

One afternoon, Charulata dishes with the Poet about all the beautiful women in her favorite author's books. She curls her lip when she names one of them, Lutfunessa—Arabic for "grace of women"—and describes her as plain, dark-skinned, thin-lipped, not-as-pretty-as-the-others. (Her problematic fave author is Bankim Chandra Chatterjee, the novelist and the composer of "Vande Mataram," impassioned song of the Swadeshi movement to free India. To this day, the tune lives on as a Hindu nationalist anthem that represents the right-wing, fascist factions of India.)

Bankim represented the essence of the Bengali *bhadralok*, the people of Charulata and the Poet's economic class. He dreamt of a Hindu *rashtra*, India as a Hindu homeland, free from British rule. His writing—lauded for its lyricism—crackled with disdain for Muslims. His words were powerful enough to influence the first Partition of Bengal, a foreshadowing of the ultimate, and terribly violent, Partition of India in 1947, which would split South Asia into India and Pakistan. It makes sense that a woman of Charulata's class and caste would read Bankim's work. Despite the ways I related to her character, a young writer caught like a caged bird between wifehood and sexual longing who escapes into books, I kept wondering: *Where are my people in this film about wealthy Bengal Brahmins from West Bengal living on giant estates?*

Lutfunessa, the dark-skinned, unpretty character in Bankim's work, is the sole Muslim woman, a ghost in this work of art. This Muslim woman could be from East Bengal, which would become East Pakistan and, ultimately, Bangladesh. This woman had the same name as my *dadi*, my paternal grandmother. Lutfunessa. Our ancestral narratives remain partitioned in a spectral *zenana*, lost in the inner, inner chambers of the upper-caste *bhadralok* consciousness. From their perspective, you'd never know that Muslim women were writers or dreamers, because their loves, heartbreaks, and sexual desires never made the final cut.

. . .

And so, I wonder, what became of Charulata?

After her husband witnesses her crying wildly for the Poet, he rides around aimlessly in a carriage, distraught. He returns home, and Charulata reaches her hand out to him. "Esho," she says. ("Come.") Satyajit Ray's use of still photographs represents the last moments we see Charulata and her husband. Reaching for each other. Holding hands. Staring off into the middle distance—an impasse. The possibility of a future. Did Charulata's marriage ever become bearable, or even joyous? Did she and her husband ever start their magazine together? Did they have a child? Did she become a young widow? Did she commit suicide?

. . .

After the screening of Ray's film, another decade passed before I read Bangladeshi characters in English (albeit British ones) in Zadie

Smith's *White Teeth*. Fiction by non-Black and non-Indigenous people of color is oft centered on the immigrant narrative, and within the South Asian diaspora, the dominant culture of Indian, upper-caste, and Hindu is the story centered over and over again. And in modern film and television, where there is undeniably more representation of South Asians than when I was growing up, still these stories are centered on the experiences of Indians and Indian Americans. South Asians from Bangladesh, Pakistan, Sri Lanka, Nepal, or Bhutan are rarely a part of the narrative; we are invisible Indians.

What does it mean to write at the edges? What does it mean to be diaspora, stripped of the unreasonable project of universality, and instead be intensely committed to decolonization and decentering hegemony, all the while crackling with sensuality and rage?

* * *

I am the child of Bangladeshi immigrants who arrived less than a decade after the Liberation War in 1971, a final Partition of East and West Pakistan. I am their firstborn daughter, raised in the South and the Midwest before we finally settled in New York. But I'm writing an experience that is not theirs, an experience that is still emerging into the American consciousness. In the States, Muslim voices, art, and lives celebrated by dominant cultural imagination are oft required to mute or diminish their overt Muslimness. We are asked to deny our historic and lived relationship to imperialism, violence, and erasure, especially post 9/11. I know the shame of hiding the truest parts of me—during the Gulf War, my parents warned me never to tell strangers our last name, Islam—these parts that complicate an Asian American or South Asian American identity: I am Muslim. I am Bangladeshi. I am American. As I am a non-Indian Bangladeshi

Muslim, the pain of my brownness is not just that I am invisible to white or Black people; it is that my people—Muslims—are considered to be difficult, dangerous, dissenting, the world over. Not only by white people, but by our own South Asian kin. Writing the narratives of Muslim women and femmes is not merely about representation. Writing defies the silencing of our truths, eschews any flattening. We are not oppressed, silent and broken by violence. Writing ourselves in our fullness and complexity gives us a future. Our foremothers—*Lutfunessa*—were never imagined as a part of history, even though their stories are older than any nation.

My dad's from that generation like a lot of immigrants where he feels like if you come to this country, you pay this thing like the American dream tax, right? Like, you're going to endure some racism. And if it doesn't cost you your life, well, hey, you lucked out. Pay it. There you go, Uncle Sam. But for me, like a lot of us, I was born here. So I actually had the audacity of equality.

—HASAN MINHAJ

The Ring

by Amna Nawaz

I could feel his stare before I turned my head to confirm it.

He was seated on the DC Metro. Suit and tie. Briefcase at his feet. Newspaper raised, but just below his nose. His eyes were trained on me. On my hand, wrapped around the metal pole. On my ring—a small turquoise pinky ring, with black calligraphy. *Bismillah hir Rahman nir Rahim* (In the name of God, the most gracious, the most merciful). A gift from my grandmother.

His eyes met mine and narrowed slightly. But I was the one who looked away quickly, embarrassed and scared. My mind raced. *Was he going to say something? Do something? Does he think I'm one of "them"?*

I turned the ring around, moving the script to my palm side. At my stop, I quickly exited the car, glancing back over my shoulder. He was staring at me again, newspaper still slightly raised. I turned and hurried into work, cheeks burning and heart racing.

He thinks I'm one of them.

It was just days after the 9/11 attacks. I was twenty-one. Fresh out of college, on my first job as a journalist, and people who looked like me and claimed my faith as their own had just committed a heinous act of mass murder. People who looked like me and my family were under suspicion and assault. They were being yelled at. Spit on. Some were beaten, shot, and killed. Whether or not I belonged here, in the only country I'd ever called home, was now up for scrutiny.

In that moment on the subway, I did something I went on to do countless times over the years that followed. As prolonged stares and random security checks became the norm and "Where are you *really* from?" carried new weight, I hid part of myself, quieted part of myself, minimized part of myself. I did all this to avoid the scrutiny, the questions, and the hostility of others. I did it to avoid being yelled at, spit on, or attacked. I turned the ring around, over and over again.

It took years and years before I realized how deeply ingrained I'd allowed this survival technique to become. Deflecting casual racism, laughing off the discomfort of others, dismissing their ignorance— these were skills I developed early and practiced daily. My parents are from Pakistan. Like a lot of first-generation American kids, I learned to occupy the space between two very different, sometimes-conflicting worlds. I learned to be polite but not submissive. Assertive but not confrontational. I was encouraged to ask questions, but respect authority. And it was these lessons, underscored by a new fear of being targeted, that rang through my ears in the days after 9/11. Who was I, as a young, Brown Muslim woman, to call you out for staring? Who was I, to question your decision to pull me aside and pat me down in public? Who was I, to call out your racism, your xenophobia, your Islamophobia, for what it is?

Growing up in the 1980s and 1990s in Virginia, we were the others, one of the only families of color in my cul-de-sac and school and on my sports teams. Those were overwhelmingly white circles where we spent most of our time, and the microaggressions piled up over the years. The neighbors who couldn't say or spell our names. The parents who wouldn't talk to mine in the waiting room for a school interview. The condescension of others when they detected an accent in your speech.

My mother, graceful and determined, would dismiss these moments with a flick of her wrist and a simple "silly people." My father, an erudite man of few words, went so far as to once refer to them as "stupid people," uncharacteristically strong language that made my sisters and me giggle. We didn't talk about these incidents much growing up, because they were deemed not worthy of our time or attention. Why give them oxygen. Why grant them power over you. What my parents were teaching us was to not let these moments stop us. To find a way around them, rather than fighting through them. That was how we survived.

At the same time, my parents worked hard for us to stay connected to the parts of our story that defined us. We spoke Urdu in the house. We kept a tight circle of Pakistani friends, who were like our family here in the States—Aunties and Uncles to whom we have no blood relation. When I complained about having to sit through the recitation of the Our Father every Wednesday at school during chapel services (my parents sent me to an all-girl Episcopalian school because it was the best available education), my mother told me to just quietly recite my own Muslim prayer under my breath.

I learned to survive in the world as it was. I minimized parts of myself that challenged or confused others. I wore the ring—I just kept it to myself.

Back then, there was little sense among South Asians of collective identity or community across all Asian Americans. What did someone with family roots in India have in common with someone who traced their heritage to China? What did the traditions and experiences of Vietnamese Americans have to do with Bangladeshi Americans? When we checked boxes on school or health forms, we generally checked "Other" and then specified: "Pakistani American."

Over the last twenty years, that's changed. There is a sense of shared history, of common experiences and memories. The understanding has taken hold that in a moment the country you call home can turn on you because of your faith, the shape of your eyes, the land where your ancestors are buried. It can deny you entry, as it did in 1882. It can round you up and imprison you en masse, as it did in 1942. Its tolerance can turn to suspicion in the blink of an eye, as it did after 9/11. The country you've always loved will not always love you back.

Knowing what I know now, it doesn't take much to connect the past to the present. America wanted Chinese workers to help build the railroads, then branded Chinese women prostitutes and banned them from entering the United States with the Page Act of 1875. Nearly 150 years later, a white man targets, shoots, and kills Asian women in the Atlanta area, claiming a sexual addiction drove him to do it. In the early 1900s, thousands of South Asian men came to the United States and were met with an onslaught of mockery, discrimination, and ultimately another immigration law in 1917 barring their entry. Over eighty years later, Brown people across America—anyone who looked Muslim, whether they were Sikh, Hindu, Christian, or any other faith—are targeted in a surge of anti-Muslim attacks after 9/11.

I never learned about these moments in school. I was left to discover them as an adult. Left to draw my own connections between the way we were and the way we are. And what it will take to change that.

My children today are a product of their time, just as I was back then. And they will navigate their own paths of self-identity and perception, as biracial American women raised by a Brown, Muslim mom and white, Christian dad. They were too young to know about the kitchen table conversations their father and I had when talk of a Muslim registry was in the news. They are still too young to know about the flood of hate mail and social media comments I receive regularly, calling for my deportation or worse and deriding me as "ungrateful" in expletive-fueled messages. But my girls are growing up aware of a broader version of history than I was taught. A truer version.

They will know that Muslims were among the earliest enslaved people brought to this country at its founding. That the South Asian part of our family's ability to choose this country as our home rested on the Black-led civil rights work of the 1950s and 1960s. That the sentiment driving the surge in anti-Asian incidents in the 2020s is as old as the nation itself.

They learned to read as George Floyd's name appeared in headlines spread across our kitchen table. They see Americans of all shades and backgrounds marching for Black lives on the news. Their parents send them out to run in the sun, unhindered by the inherent anti-Blackness that led my own grandmother to discourage me from playing sports for fear my skin would get too dark (my mother, quietly, dismissed those concerns and told me to ignore them).

My girls will know our collective stories, our collective experiences, and our collective hope. Among Asian Americans, someone, at some point in our family history, chose to call this country home. They chose to believe that America could be as good and great as she says she is. My girls will know the work it takes, and will continue to take, for their generation and the next, to make that true for everyone.

They will not hide the parts of themselves that confuse or challenge others.

I wonder today, if I'd been empowered with this same sense of history and understanding twenty years ago, what I might have said or done differently on that subway. If I would've held his gaze. Confronted him in the moment. Asked what he was starting at. If I would've more forcefully fought through the moments of racism in my education and career in the years that followed, rather than trying to navigate around them. If I would've felt safe enough to stop minimizing those parts of myself to survive.

I wear a new prayer ring today, a gift from my mother. It's slightly broader than the previous one. More prominent. Two-toned, in gold and silver. The inscription is the same—*Bismillah hir Rahman nir Rahim*. In the name of God, the most gracious, the most merciful. I wear it every day, facing out.

a bad day

by Catzie Vilayphonh

a bad day,

they say,

starts on the wrong side of bed

I was born in a refugee camp,

so I must've woken up on the wrong side of war,

the wrong side of history,

the wrong side of foreign policy

afterwards,

my family

resettled

on the wrong side of America,

on the wrong side of the neighborhood,

where i attended the wrong side of school,

i learned

the shape of my eyes
the sounds for my name
the food in my lunch box
were all on the wrong side
the country my parents were born,
on the wrong side of the world,
published on the wrong side of the books
even when I could pronounce those English words so perfectly,
it wasn't right
it wasn't white,
so still it was
wrong
wrong
wrong

wrong place, wrong time
take it on the Chin,
like my first name was Vincent
quietly forget I existed
like Spike Lee did Yuri Kochiyama
laugh it off like when
that white comedian said
"i love chinks"
and followed up with
"What kind of a world do we live in where a totally cute white girl
    can't say 'chink' on network television?"

(that was Sarah Silverman btw)
even our racial slurs are a joke
there's always laughing
when you're waiting on the apology
"I'm sorry" is always pronounced wrong
when they don't really mean it

or they just give up
just like my teachers did over roll call
just like your coworkers did over coffee
just like our news media did over the weekend

so
let's speak our names out loud
let's speak our names out loud
let's speak our names out loud

there's nothing wrong if
you want me to remind you
which lunar animal it is this year
or say what day in April
Southeast Asian new year will fall on
nothing wrong
if you want to see cultural dances
and I just want blessings from Buddhist monks

nothing wrong with you talking about
Muslim bans and Chinese Exclusion Acts
or if I bring up Vietnam and want to include Myanmar
or deportations of Cambodian Americans
nothing wrong with
discussing the differences between
internment camps
and refugee camps
fancy Asians and jungle Asians
nothing wrong with
conversations about soy sauce, sambal, sriracha,
or that you like the way I say *sriracha*
there's nothing wrong
if you want to celebrate Bruce Lee
and I want to remember my father
if you tell me I'm beautiful in your language
and I don't tell you how I say *thank you* in mine

nothing wrong if
you want to
understand
be more informed
say it right
be supportive
be here

ok,
ok,
ok,
but maybe
not today,
maybe today
is the wrong day

today
we honor their passing,
invoke their spirits as ancestors joining ours,
and speak their names out loud:
Vicha Ratanapakdee
Xiaojie Tan
Daoyou Feng
Hyun Jung Grant
Suncha Kim
Soon Chung Park
Yong Ae Yue

today
was a bad day

Fourteen Ways of Being Asian in America over Thirty-Six Years

by Melissa de la Cruz

1. 1985, San Francisco

I am fourteen years old and walking to the BART train in San Francisco with my twelve-year-old sister. We are in our school uniforms. On her: blazer, white button-down shirt, gray skirt, knee socks, navy-and-white Oxfords, hair in pigtails. On me: white button-down shirt, gray skirt, burgundy sweater, scrunched-down socks, penny loafers. Our uniforms are ill fitting and awkward, whereas they fit our classmates perfectly. We learn much later that most of them had the standard uniforms *tailored*.

We are scholarship students in America, whereas our family used to endow scholarships at our private school in Manila. We have just moved to this country from the Philippines. After a sheltered life of being chauffeured around in a Mercedes to and from school, we now have to make the grueling commute from the city to the suburbs, which means a crowded public bus, then the BART train, then another bus. We moved here for a better life, my parents said.

Market Street is the only place in America we have ever seen people who are homeless in this country. They are usually slovenly bearded young white guys. We do our best to avoid them, crossing the street or trying not to make eye contact.

Today, I accidentally make eye contact with a homeless guy checking us out. "MOTHERFUCKING CHINKS! GO BACK TO YOUR COUNTRY!" he spits at us. My sister and I pick up the pace; we don't look at him, and we don't yell back. We just hurry, backpacks over our shoulders, into the train station.

Go back to our country? Doesn't he know how much we want to?

2. 1989, New York

When I am a student at Columbia University, my only dream is to go to nightclubs. The hottest club in 1989 is called Mars. As my friends and I worry about the "face police" and whether we will make it past the velvet ropes, someone assures us we will. "Rudolph's main girl there is Asian—she loves Asian girls. She'll let you in."

There is a huge line outside the club, but we are beckoned to the front. There are four of us. The doorman lifts the rope.

I look up, and there is the most beautiful Japanese girl, sitting on a stool above the crowd and holding a clipboard. She is wearing tiny denim shorts and a baseball cap pulled low over her forehead, an outfit I will replicate for years to come. She makes eye contact and nods. I have never felt more like I belonged anywhere in my life. We are inside. Success!

The club is empty. We have the time of our lives.

3. 1993, New York

"You're friends with the two Asian girls who sit in the front?" a girl asks a friend of mine our senior year of college. My friend is white, as is the girl who asks, as is her boyfriend. But I know their names: Erika and Sean. But to her, my best friend, Jennie, and I, we are nameless. We are just "the two Asian girls who sit in the front."

4. 1994, New York

My friends and I go see the fireworks at the harbor for the Fourth of July. The crowd is massive, and we are lost in the sea of people. I hear someone talking about me. "Dang, I didn't know Asian girls could look like that." He whistles. I think it was meant to be a compliment. I don't know whether to blush or to slap him.

5. 1996, New York

My boyfriend, who is blond and from New Hampshire, tells me he is breaking up with me because I'm Asian and he doesn't want to be seen as the kind of guy with an "Asian fetish" since his last years-long relationship was with a Chinese girl.

I am gobsmacked (even though I haven't read Harry Potter yet). "You're breaking up with me because I'm Asian and you don't want to be seen as racist?"

"Yes," he replies.

He married a white woman. I googled them.

6. 1996, New York

I interrogate my new boyfriend, who is blond and from Ohio, about the races of the girls he dated in the past. Two of his girlfriends were white; one of them was Asian. He is very different from my last boyfriend. For one, he is very wise and mature, even though he is three years younger than I am.

When we get married, he tells me that it never occurred to him to remark upon my race.

"What did you think I was?" I ask.

"A New Yorker," he answers.

7. 2002, Pasadena

After the wedding, we visit my parents. My dad suggests that I take my husband's last name to sell more books. I tell him he is wrong.

I am right.

8. 2005, Los Angeles

My husband is renovating our new house in the hills. He moves his office and desk out to the top of the driveway. Neighbors stop and say hi; he tells me that everyone is so friendly. In the twelve years I lived in that house, I met no neighbors. No one said hi to me or acknowledged me in any way.

9. 2006, Palm Springs

I am at the Parker Palm Springs with my baby. She is chubby and blond and milky and delicious. She looks exactly like my husband. At the pool, someone points to her and asks, "Is that YOUR baby?" I nod. This is my baby. This white baby came out of this Asian body. I am not the nanny. I am her mom.

10. 2009, Pasadena

When my dad dies, friends from all over the country and the world come to his funeral. My dad was very popular. He was an anchorman for the local Filipino TV station and a "star" in the Philippines. In college, he sang a cappella and was in a band. He and his friends and their cool priest professor would get together on Fridays to drink; they became known as the "Bottoms Up" crew. My dad was the life of the party. Every time I read about withdrawn, angry Asian men in fiction, I feel sad that people think all Asian dads are like that.

Anyway, a lot of people at the funeral hand sympathy cards to my mom. When it is over, my mom opens them to find checks or cash. "Oh!" my mom says. "I forgot that in Filipino culture, people help pay for the funeral." The gift of helping. The gift of community. She has lived in America so long she has forgotten our customs. Mom puts the money toward my dad's headstone. When we look at it, we think of all his friends who loved him, and we are consoled.

11. 2010, Palm Springs

My husband and I buy a vacation house in Palm Springs. It once belonged to Bill Lear, the founder of Lear Jets. I happily wear caftans and no makeup, a reprieve from the glamour of Los Angeles. We invite friends to come and visit often. One day, I open the door to a friend's mom and dad, who are older, from the Midwest, and very wealthy. They think I am the maid. I am not.

12. 2014, San Diego

My husband takes our daughter, who looks like him, to Comic-Con. She's dressed as Harley Quinn. He made her a hammer, so they have to go through "Weapons Check" to ensure it's just made out of cardboard. They get stopped all the time by people who tell them how cute she is. He hands her off to me to go to his panel. I walk the entire floor with my daughter. No one talks to me or tells me how cute she is.

13. 2019, Los Angeles

DC Comics calls to tell me they are reimagining iconic DC characters for their new YA graphic novel line and want me to contribute. At this point in my career, I have launched several hit franchises—The Au Pairs, Blue Bloods, Witches of East End, Alex & Eliza, and, most recently, The Descendants, about Disney's iconic villains.

I am intrigued, but it is not an easy "yes" on my part. While I am more than familiar with Batman, Superman, Wonder Woman, et al., they don't hold as close a place in my heart as, say, Maleficent and Cruella de Vil or the Lord of the Rings books. (Full disclosure: Marvel's X-Men are my favorite superheroes.)

As I am considering the opportunity, I have another conversation with the big cheese at DC Comics. They tell me that everyone they've brought on board thus far is doing a smaller superhero, but they really want someone to tackle the marquee names.

And then they ask me to reimagine Batman for a YA audience.

Batman. I'd be working with Bruce Wayne, because as a teenager, he's not Batman yet. But still, one of the biggest superheroes of all time. I ask them . . . could I make Bruce Wayne Asian? As I speak to them, my mind races: *What if Bruce Wayne's fortune came from his mother, a wealthy Hong Kong socialite? What if Alfred wasn't his butler, but his savvy, cosmopolitan gay uncle? What if . . . What if . . .* And I get excited. I am excited because I'd never read an iconic American superhero who had my background. I'm Filipino-Chinese-Spanish, and more Chinese than Filipino or Spanish. My brother and his family live in Hong Kong. My mom was something of a Manila socialite. I pitch my vision of a crazy rich Asian Bruce Wayne. They love it. *I* love it. I am on board.

As the graphic novel's publication date approaches, DC starts promoting it. They release a *Gossip Girl*–like trailer—that's when the hate starts. Hatred that Batman has been dragged into the YA space. Hatred that Batman is Asian. I am shocked, and scared, and furious. Within hours, trolls leave ugly and disgusting comments on my Instagram and on Twitter. I write for little kids, as well, so I am mostly concerned about my younger readers seeing this language.

That very day, I lock my social media for a month. I don't want to draw attention to the hate mail, so I decide to ignore it. But it leaves me shaking and scared—I have never experienced anything like that before. One day of it is enough.

Just thinking about it now makes me weep. I wished I'd never written the book. And that makes me sad, because I wanted to write that book because I wanted to show that anyone—of any background—can be a superhero. That we don't have to be relegated to the sidekick or the best friend. We can be in the spotlight. We can be Batman.

In the aftermath of the trolling, I was quiet. I was quiet because I was ashamed. Just my existence was enough for these so-called fans to hate me. But I'm going to talk about it now, not because I am suddenly brave, but because if we don't talk about it, no one will know what it's really like to be Asian in America.

14. Los Angeles, 2020

My fourteen-year-old daughter walks around H Mart with me, excitedly stuffing boba ice cream and dumplings into our cart. "Mom, you're not Asian enough! How come we never come here?"

I tell her that when I moved to the United States at her age in the 1980s we were embarrassed to be seen eating strange, weird-smelling food. That my best friend, who is Korean, did the same thing, and to this day her favorite food is peanut butter. That it was all about trying to fit in, trying to get people to forget you were different.

She shrugs as she puts ube ice cream in the cart. "It's cool to be Asian."

Why We Don't Always Fight

by Edmund Lee

I recall a night from my preteen years, before the crisis of self-awareness sets in and rattles your very identity. My family is out to dinner. My parents, who emigrated from South Korea before I was born, had embraced all things American with a certain jingoistic fervor, and that evening we went out to a Pizza Hut in the suburbs of Long Island. This is the late seventies.

As we were waiting to be seated, it became clear we were being ignored. Several patrons who entered after us were immediately given tables. My father asked to speak to the manager, and with a raised voice he asked why we hadn't been offered seats. The manager, who looked to be a teenager, sized up my father's evident rage and sighed. He pointed to a booth and we sat down. As the waitress handed us menus, she looked befuddled, almost as if to say, *I guess we're doing this?*

Our order took forever, far longer than those who came after us. When the food finally arrived, it was burnt to a crisp. My parents were livid. My younger sister and I sensed a pending calamity and we slumped lower in the booth.

The tin fury in both my parents' voices rang through the restaurant. My father pointed to the charred circle of dough and cheese and said, "This is how you serve us!?" He screamed about being mistreated, that—and here it came, the word—this was "racist." Everyone stared. A man at the table next to us told my father to simmer down. The manager protested. Then he took a jab. We were "difficult customers from the start," he said. My father's face, normally a deep shade of brown, a peasant brown, turned red. He stood up, looked at my mother, my sister, and me, and said we were leaving.

I couldn't look at anyone, including my parents. But when we got into the car, I yelled at my father about why he had caused such a fuss. Until that moment, we had been blissful citizens of the suburban middle, the pleasant, hidden center. Now, somehow, my father's outburst had cracked open our very place in this universe. We were, all of a sudden, outsiders. Nonparticipants. Other. (The truth, I soon learned, is we always were.)

He turned around and looked at my sister and me. "What they did was wrong," he said firmly. "That's not how we should be treated. I want you to remember this and whenever something like this happens you have to say something. Don't ever keep quiet. You have to fight."

I looked away. I was starving and upset. But more than that I was unsettled about who I was, of my place in the collective, such as it were, which at the time meant the mostly white enclaves of an outlying district of New York City in the twilight of the 1970s.

In the tale of race relations, it's a minor incident, perhaps a handful of words in a saga dominated by two massive ruptures in the founding of this country: the genocide of Native Americans and the enslavement and continued killings of Black Americans.

But when I got to college and found my Asian American cipher, I discovered just how rare that moment was. My friends' parents didn't always make a fuss. That's not to say they didn't know when they were being mistreated. But immigrants often don't report such incidents, or rage at racism. Many are undocumented. Many don't speak English. My father had the advantage of speech, of citizenship and a rare ethnic disposition all Koreans will recognize as an anger incarnate (that's another essay).

For decades, Asian Americans have only come together in moments of crisis. The killing of Vincent Chin in 1982, for example. And in March 2021 the killings in Atlanta. We've always been a fractured state. We speak different languages, worship various religions, are politically diverse (or divided), and have the largest wealth gap in the nation. We are a phantom identity.

Even the rise in violence against Asian Americans over the past few years—tied to the pandemic and Donald Trump's use of a frequent refrain: "the China virus"—has been cast into doubt as a unifying moment. Before the Atlanta killings, the writer Jay Caspian Kang made the case that it wasn't entirely clear that there has been an actual surge in anti-Asian crimes, or that Trump somehow was the trigger, especially since some of the suspected perpetrators were Black. He fails to consider the possibility that even non–Trump supporters might buy into his rhetoric and blame Asian Americans for the pandemic. If we only exist in times of friction and we can't even agree on a signal moment of brutality, do we exist at all? I mean, what are we fighting?

In a February 2021 essay, the writer Hua Hsu said: "It's difficult to describe anti-Asian racism when society lacks a coherent, historical account of what that racism actually looks like." Our "victimhood," as he describes it, lacks a vernacular.

The killings in Atlanta—six of the eight murdered were Asian women—would seem to offer a trenchant record, even carve the words "anti-Asian violence" onto a granite stele as a kind of universal marker from which the rest of the world could learn. The Atlanta Police Department, citing the perpetrator's words, attributed his violence to an attempt to rid himself of his temptations. The alleged killer, an evangelical white male who had a "sex addiction," put a bullet in the faces of several of the women. In May, almost two months after the killings, the police ruled it was a hate crime.

Even the outpouring of protests, the words of President Biden, and the latest headlines describing the rise in anti-Asian attacks seem to have been cast in parallel to Atlanta. The yawning gap between the official record and the distress Asian Americans feel in their bones is mind-numbingly frustrating. It's exhausting. It also mirrors the stunted, disconnected aspect of the Asian American identity itself. We seem to phase in and out of existence, often at the mercy of other people's doubt.

Atlanta quashed any wavering among Asian Americans. In the days after the murders, I received emails and texts from my Asian American friends, some of whom I hadn't heard from in years, asking, telling in some variation, "Hey, I'm here. You okay?" like a Bat signal. But the clarity of the moment was best summed up by a seventy-five-year-old woman named Xiao Zhen Xie, who was attacked on the streets of San Francisco, just a day after the shootings in Atlanta, by a thirty-nine-year-old man. She was sucker-punched, but then she picked up a wooden plank and beat him to the point where he had to be carried away on a stretcher. A GoFundMe page started by her grandson to help with medical expenses raised over $1,000,000, but she insisted it all go to the Asian American community to combat racism. There's no other way to say it: she's a badass.

There are competing threads of Asian Americanness. They tend to manifest along two lines. At one end, there's a conservative tug, one that leans into a kind of ethnic nationalism, the "I want what's mine" brigade, who care less about a broader collective. This is the same group that aligned itself with white conservatives in a recent legal suit against Ivy League universities in an effort to unwind affirmative action. Within this strain, arguably, are those who have also called for greater policing presence in the wake of anti-Asian violence.

It's a troubling congregation. Their actions have created a wedge within Asian America and between Asian Americans and others, in particular Black Americans, a community who are met with the threat of violence every day, especially from law enforcement. The shock Asian Americans felt from Atlanta is a daily one for them.

But at the other end, there's a more progressive strain, one that is more tightly aligned with Black Americans and other minority groups and sees white supremacy as the root of the problem. This group tends to be younger. My daughter, a third-generation Asian American, who has led protests for more racial inclusivity at her high school, is one such card-carrying comrade.

But in either case, the Asian American persona only seems to come into focus at moments of friction, and if a hate crime can't be called a hate crime the friction itself loses substance.

There's another wrinkle. As elderly Asian Americans were beaten and spit on and Asian American schoolchildren were bullied and belittled, the Academy Awards committee announced several Oscar nominations, including Best Picture, for the indie film *Minari*, a quiet and moving story about a Korean American family trying to make it in America. Let me be clear, I'm not making a case for representational politics, which is its own thorny media game.

You may find it ironic, or perhaps self-hating, to know that I was disappointed by the attention placed on this film. It's a wonderful piece of art, but I couldn't help but feel skeptical of the official accolades, which often come from a misplaced sense of authenticity, that Asian Americans can only come alive when portrayed as striving newcomers. My daughter, who found little connection to the story, calls such preoccupations (not the film) "white gaze trauma porn."

How can a nation at one moment pour hate on a group while in the next acknowledge their lives through the country's highest cultural honor? (You know we all still live for the movies.) Not too long ago, the white-hot success of *Crazy Rich Asians*, the rise (and fall) of NBA player Jeremy Lin, and the scores of Asian American comics landing Netflix specials seemed to signal a pop culture moment, a critical flash point for a group that's usually invisible.

In truth, none of these examples—throw in K-pop and 2020's Oscar winner *Parasite*, even though they're not Asian American so much as instances of Asian Americana by proxy—are wholly authentic. They're bits and pieces, take-it-off-the-shelf whatnots you can patch into an identity. I remember the wave of Hong Kong films that started entering American cinemas in the 1990s, specifically the John Woo epics that redefined the gangster genre with flamboyant displays of violence. I latched on to them as somehow representational, even though I was not from Hong Kong or Chinese. Or a gangster. But it didn't matter. It spoke to me.

In other words, Asian America can be a postmodern identity when it's not forced into being by the threat of violence. There's something potentially powerful, and unifying, in these quieter flashes of media recognition. Perhaps that is the vernacular we ought to be seeking.

There is still a deep history of silence among Asian Americans, of keeping out of the way. It's partly cultural, but it's driven more by a white narrative that submission, that following the rules, or not making a fuss, will get you ahead. It was given a name by President George Bush: "model minority."

Despite the potent events behind Atlanta, I worry we will once again check out after some time has passed.

And so, I will always return to how my father perceived that night. He decided to turn an uncivil moment, an incident of racism, into a real thing simply by giving it a name. He spoke it into existence. Only as an adult did I recognize that his outburst was in fact a brave act of creation. It forced me to acknowledge my difference, my distance from the false center I thought I inhabited, and gave me an identity.

But as we drove away, I heard something else, a moment of doubt. Mumbling under his breath, my father said, "I don't know, maybe I made a mistake."

Dad, you didn't.

I only care if my mom is proud of me.

—BRETMAN ROCK

A Pair of Shorts

by Kao Kalia Yang

Every time I see a pair of shorts on a girl with thin legs, an Asian American girl, I think of my Hmong self, my mother, and my grandmother. Grandma passed away in 2003 when I was twenty-two years old. In fact, it was her passing that sent me on a chase for her life story and on the path into writing. Nearly twenty years later, I cannot help but think of her, my mother, and myself when we were new in America, seen and treated as outsiders, and how fervently we tried in our different ways to make our lives possible here together. Memories rise inside of me and I'm a child again.

It's almost summer now. The days have grown hot underneath the bright sun. The dandelion flowers, once yellow pops across the hillside, have turned white with age. The flowering trees have dropped their petals. On the sidewalks, the petals have stained the patches of concrete in patterns of brown where people have walked and run, danced and jumped—despite the fact that their blooms had been pink, purple, and white.

Underneath my long skirt, in our small townhouse, my legs feel hampered and heavy already, despite the fact that it is still only morning. I sneak the pair of shorts into my backpack; I'm so nervous my hands shake. My mother couldn't care less. She's the one who got me the pair of pink shorts—tight at the waist but that balloon around my thighs—from the church basement lady. But my grandmother cares a whole lot. How many times has she seen my scrawny refugee girl legs, bruised at the shins, and said, "Kalia, why do you wear underwear outside?! Go get a pair of pants or a skirt. Now, please go. I don't want to see my granddaughter in her underwear, and the world shouldn't have to either."

In the past, when my mother is around and my grandmother has said such things to me, my mother would respond, "Oh, Mother, Kalia is just a child. Even I, a grown woman, wear shorts sometimes!" Or on the occasions when she has said nothing, my mother later assures me, "It's fine, Kalia. You can wear shorts if you want to. I think you look cute in them."

I want to please both of them, my mother and my grandmother. But I also want to look like the other kids at school, the ones whose legs climb into the sky when they swing high and move fast ahead of me after the balls in the school yard. So, instead of wearing the pink shorts and walking down the stairs like normal and going to school like normal, I sneak the pair of shorts into my backpack and act as normally as I can.

Dawb, my older sister, is already at the kitchen table. She's wearing her blue-and-black dress, the one with a flounce across her thin middle, and although she's only in third grade, she looks like she's ready to go to work. She's eating her half of the Wai Wai noodles my mother has made for our breakfast. My half is in a bowl, tendrils of steam coming from it. I know I have to hurry so we don't miss the school bus. I sit down and I grab the pair of chopsticks and tackle the noodles, savoring the salty broth and the curled noodles. By the time I'm done, Dawb is already waiting for me by the door.

Our bus stop is only a short walk away from our front door with its familiar *C*, but Grandma walks us and waits until we get on the bus. She sits in the shade of an American elm in the already humid morning and picks at the blades of grass with her hands as she watches over us. We stand at the back of the line of children, other refugee children like us from Cambodia and Vietnam, a few Black children, and other Hmong children.

Grandma visits us once a year in Minnesota from California. She comes in the beginning of the summer, stays through the hot months, and then leaves with the fall. Other children in the projects have grandmothers and grandfathers year-round. We don't. It is special when she visits. We are lucky we have a grandma who can walk us to the bus stop and wait for the bus to come.

As I watch her, my grandmother acts like the sun isn't already heating up the earth. She wears a fake fur hat. She has a black sweater on top of a flowering shirt. Her dark skirt is long. Her feet are clad in black canvas shoes. Her ankles are bare and brown. The skin of her eyelids falls over the corners of her eyes, and the wrinkles fan out like the rays of the sun I draw on the corners of all my papers. She is not smiling at us, but her only tooth shows anyways, and I love her so much I feel the warmth that she doesn't climb up my neck from my chest.

My grandmother has had a hard life. Her parents died when she was just a girl. She had to raise her younger siblings in the house of an uncle. In that house, she was barely a woman when she was married off to my grandfather, a widower with no children. After nine children, my grandfather died. My grandmother was left to raise the children on her own in a small country caught up in a big war. Beneath the rain of bullets, she led them into lives as young men and women. When the war was over and genocide was declared against my people for helping the Americans, she had to leave everything she knew behind in Laos. In the refugee camps of Thailand, she waited for a life elsewhere. Now here we were in America, living in the housing projects, living on welfare, trying to be normal.

Ye announces, "The bus is here!" She is my friend. She's only six and I'm seven. She's far wealthier than I am, though she lives in the projects too. She is an only child. Her grandparents own a gold jewelry store. She's Vietnamese but born in America. On her wrists, she wears real gold bangles. Around her neck, she has not one but two gold chains of differing lengths. Her hair is always done in a fancy way; today, she has it tied in high buns on either side of her head, perfectly parted in the middle.

Grandma waves by holding her right hand above her head. She moves the whole hand quickly like she's making wind. Dawb and I both run to give her a fast hug before racing to the back of the bus line.

On the bus, I sit next to Ye. I'm by the window. I wave to Grandma, who is now on her feet and standing on the sidewalk, by putting both my hands to the glass and moving them like windshield wipers on either side of my face. My grandmother looks lonely in the sunshine, a small figure of a small woman caught out of the seasons in her warm clothes. I wish she would take off her sweater so she could be more comfortable in the hot day, but also so she would look more like other people's grandmothers.

When the bus starts moving, my hands reach for the zipper of my backpack. They shake as I take out the pair of shorts. I feel like I am betraying my grandmother. I look around me. There are lots of kids in shorts and T-shirts.

I whisper, "Ye, be my lookout while I put on the shorts underneath my skirt."

The white kids who get on the bus before the housing project kids find everything we do odd. They say so all the time. When we are eating Asian Jell-O candy in the cups, they say, "Ewww." When we share our ghost stories with one another, they sometimes point and laugh and say, "Ghosts don't exist." I don't want to be caught putting on shorts; I don't want them to say anything to me. But the process of putting on shorts under your skirt without standing up is hard, as the bus is unsteady. I nearly fall, hitting the seat in front of me.

The boy in front of me feels the impact of my body against the back of his seat and yells to the bus driver, "This Hmong girl is not sitting like she should!"

Heat erupts on my face. I'm red and shrinking in the seat, both my ankles caught in the shorts. Ye has her head down. The white girls across the aisle look at us. I cringe, and my shoulders go up. The blow comes, but it is not physical. They laugh and point and say, "She's wearing shorts like underwear!"

Somewhere in the bus, I know my sister wants to come and help me, but no one is allowed to stand up on a moving bus. I hear the laughter rising all around. I sink my short nails into the rough leather of the bus seat on either side of me so I don't cry. The last thing I wanted to do was stand out.

Our bus driver, a short Hmong guy, whom the white kids make fun of and one time a Black girl knuckled on the head, a man whom we feel sorry for because he wears Chinese slippers from the kung fu movies and can barely speak English, turns on the radio. He always turns on the radio when there is commotion from the white kids.

The sound of music fills the bus and silences the laughter and somehow dispels the moment. Kids start singing along. By the time we get to the school, I have pulled the shorts on, but I don't have the courage to take the skirt off. And by the end of the school day, I come to the conclusion that it doesn't matter what I wear; I'll never fit in, be a regular American kid.

When I get home, my mother is waiting at the bus stop. Her right hand shields her eyes from the bright sun overhead. I see that her hair—long this morning, clipped in a bun—is now short. I forget myself seeing her standing there: hair to her shoulders, parted to the side, tucked behind her ears.

She says, "Do you like my hair?"

Her smile is so big and shaky, Dawb and I both answer immediately, "Yes, Niam. Yes."

She says, "Grandma disapproves. Your father cut it for me today. I got a job at the factory. They don't like people with long hair working at the factory."

Her hands reach out to us as she shrugs her shoulders.

She holds our hands in hers, and we walk together back to the brown townhouse, toward the door with the big *C* on it.

That night at dinner, we sit around the square table that came with the townhouse. The plastic is bubbling in spots, where previous families had placed their hot dishes. We are having rice again, this time with fish soup, slightly sour from tomatoes, sweet from the green onions, and spicy from the fresh chilis. We eat more fish when Grandma visits. It's easier on her single tooth.

Grandma's abnormally quiet. She won't look in my mother's direction. My father acts like everything is as it should be. My mother doesn't look at my grandmother's face when she offers the least bony portion of the fish out on her spoon toward Grandma.

Underneath the bright light from the ceiling, I look at my mother slowly. She is as beautiful as she was in the morning, only she looks younger now because her thick, long hair has been cut short like a girl's. I try to smile at her because I can sense her nervousness and fear. I notice Grandma looking at me. I smile at her, too, to let her know that everything is all right. I keep taking deep breaths between bites, telling myself, *This is my family, and this is a new place, and we are trying our best to be good to each other and survive*—knowing that underneath my skirt I have on a pair of shorts, and underneath that a pair of underwear.

Every time my seven-year-old daughter puts on a pair of shorts, I remember the way we used to be. I think of my Hmong grandmother who came to this country in the autumn of her life, too old to shift with its seasons. My Hmong American mother who came to this country young enough to compromise pieces and parts of herself so that she could work and care for her children through the harshest of seasons. And I think of myself, a girl wanting desperately to celebrate spring and summer, to be strong for her mother and her grandmother, and who tried unsuccessfully in many ways to fit in. Now that Grandma is gone, my mother is an old woman, and I am a working mother myself, it is only in my memories that we get to be together the way we were then. My Asian American girl loves shorts and T-shirts, her thin legs often darkened by bruises from her runs around me, beside me, and often ahead of me.

From the distance of nearly twenty years, I wish I could have told that young girl yearning to let her legs breathe free that all of our lives in America were just beginning, that where we were was only one part of our story. I wish I could have told her that her family was as good as they knew how to be to each other, and that in their own ways they were trying to help each other, not hurt. I want to tell the girl I used to be that these first years of her life in America would teach her how to love across space and time, to one day stand strong in her family's discomforts, and give her the power and the ability to declare them all: new Americans.

Slingshots of the Ignorant

by Aisha Sultan

I slowly head toward the school's front doors. A familiar dread rises in my chest. I won't be the only one waiting to be picked up by a parent. As expected, Michael,* with his short blond hair and arrogant sneer, is also there. We stand a distance apart among a dozen other car riders. Our parents tend to be later than the ones whose parents are already waiting in their cars when their child walks out. One by one, the other students leave. I am trapped during these moments when Michael and I are mostly alone, out of earshot from the assistant principals patrolling the grounds.

My mother didn't have idle time to wait in school pickup lines. She was constantly in motion taking care of four daughters (I was the eldest), all of whom needed to be dropped off, picked up, and fed, as

_____

* The names in this story have been changed.

well as an infant son with his constant demands. She had an endless list of chores and always seemed to be doing two things at once. She had fresh rice and hot chicken *salan* ready for us when we arrived home from school. She was either putting in another load of laundry or running the vacuum before cooking dinner for when my father got home at night. In the late afternoons, she would stand in the kitchen sautéing meat on the stove while keeping an eye on *Days of Our Lives* on the television in the family room. Maybe the soap opera reminded her of Pakistani dramas she might have seen, before an arranged marriage took her from her family to this new country.

We were the anomalies in our heavily white, Christian suburb outside of Houston, Texas. Kingwood was built as an idyllic small town right outside one of the biggest cities in the country. My parents bought a three-bedroom ranch house with orange shag carpet in a "starter" neighborhood. Across town, there were McMansions set on golf courses with views of man-made lakes.

We lived on a long street filled with other families more like us, newer to the American dream. My mom, in her hijab and broken English, did not fit in with the tennis club ladies or the social climbers in the National Charity League. We hovered between working class and the bottom rungs of middle class, but our place on that ladder was tenuous. My parents' version of health insurance rested heavily on my mom's home remedies and her relentless faith in prayers. My dad worked the long hours of a car salesman.

It was the mid-eighties, and Ronald Reagan handily had won a second term in our school mock presidential election. I had convinced my mom to buy me one of the ten-button Henley shirts from The Limited that the preppy girls wore almost daily. Mine was rose pink, and it had an Outback Red label stitched on the outside of the back neckline, so people could tell it wasn't a knock-off. It was an indulgence she couldn't afford. But my mom stretched the tight budget when she knew I longed for something out of reach. Every little bit of social capital seemed out of reach in that school.

As I clutch my books closer to my chest, I feel Michael's stare. He doesn't run with the A-list popular crowd. He isn't a well-known jock or an academic gunner. Most of my classes are with the other strivers in the honors program, but in electives like health and PE every social circle collides. I know Michael from one of those classes. He has a mean streak that looks for the weakest prey in the vicinity.

Middle school was, of course, horrid. The cafeteria was a wilderness. We sought survival in the safety of packs. By seventh grade, I found a reliable group of studious girls, who understood their supporting role in the social pecking order and were willing to take me in. But as one of the handful of brown students, a daughter of immigrants, and perhaps the only Muslim in a school of nearly a thousand students, I often felt lost in a sea of white privilege. My small circle of friends didn't insulate me from jabs from those jockeying for position. There was the snarky brunette in my journalism class who asked in front of her hangers-on every Monday if I had been to the big parties over the weekend. I had not. Passive aggression is social currency in middle school.

Michael inches closer to me on the spacious front entry after school.
"Where's your raghead mom?" he asks.
I ignore him.

"Your mom's a raghead," he says again, in case I had missed it the first time.

"Shut up, Michael."

"You all should go back to where you came from."

The tightening in my chest makes my breathing shallow. I avoid eye contact. His stocky build feels intimidating.

"Raghead. There's your raghead mom."

I shoot him a steely look as I walk away.

His words follow me as I walk toward my mom in her minivan.

In the car, I answer her questions about the day's tests or how much homework I have. In my mind, I replay the scenario from the moments before. What is his problem? I fume. Why can't he just make fun of me? I wore glasses, cheap shoes from Payless, and carried a messy stack of papers. My frizzy black hair made me stand out among the blondes. I gave him plenty of ammunition. Why is he fixated on my mom?

What was it about the hijab she wrapped around her head to cover her hair that got to him? I personally didn't care for it either. My mom exuded an effortless natural beauty. I had been in awe of her appearance for as long as I could remember. I hovered near her in the bathroom when she applied makeup to go to parties. I watched her trace liner around her large almond eyes and glide lipstick over her lips. She was the loveliest woman I had ever seen, and I could scarcely believe that my gangly, awkward self was born of her. So, I wasn't thrilled when she decided to cover her hair a few years earlier. At that age, I didn't understand why she felt compelled to hide any part of her striking appearance.

Maybe Michael's family had passed on their views about Muslims to him. Maybe it was because my mom stood out as so different in our homogenous community. All I knew was that I faced this same confrontation nearly every day and no one who may have overheard ever intervened.

As sheltered as I was by my parents, I had taken on a protective role toward my mother at a young age. She seemed so alone and out of place most days. I was powerless to protect her from the loneliness she felt from being continents away from her family. I had no way to shield her from those who would yell from their cars, "Go back to Iraq!" There was a limit to how much I could ease the burdens of the household work on her shoulders. But I would have sooner worn a hijab to school myself than reveal my daily after-school humiliation to her. Our routine at home went on without a hint of the trouble brewing at school. I never confided in a single white friend at school either.

I suppose I could have commiserated with my Muslim friends, who also came from Pakistani immigrant families, and whom I met on the weekends at our Islamic school thirty miles away. Those Friday nights and Saturday mornings in the makeshift classrooms in trailers around the mosque were a reprieve from the alienation I experienced in school. In that space, everyone was different in the same ways. My mother drove us forty minutes each way twice a week because she wanted us to be educated about our faith. For me, the religious instruction was incidental. It was the sense of belonging I craved.

I'm sure that tight-knit circle would have shared some comforting words, but it didn't cross my mind to confide in them. The weekend Islamic school was my safe zone. I left the baggage of everything that came with my brown skin in America—a name too difficult for my white peers and teachers, my superstrict parents, and insecure bullies—in Kingwood. I sure as hell wasn't going to bring Michael's taunts there.

I didn't see any point in trying to talk to a teacher; I never got the sense that they cared much about those of us on the outskirts. My health teacher called me Lisa all semester because my two-syllable name was too difficult for him. Why bother trying to confide in them. But after months of putting up with Michael's harassment, I decided to approach the adult whose job it was to handle such a situation. I knocked on Mr. Smith's door after school. He was a middle-aged man who spoke with a distinct Texan drawl and appreciated kids who didn't cause trouble. My worst offense had been a few tardies, and he had always been nice to me.

He welcomed me into his office. From behind his desk, he asked me what had brought me there.

"Michael keeps calling my mom a raghead after school," I said.

Mr. Smith nodded sympathetically and folded his hand on the desk before he leaned over and spoke. "Ah-sha," he started, mispronouncing my name. "There are gonna be people who just aren't going to like you for who you are." He didn't have to specify what he meant by who I am. We knew. "The sooner you learn to deal with it, the better off you're gonna be."

Well, okay.

I wasn't sure what sort of intervention or advice I had expected from the school guidance counselor, but this speech settled the matter in my preteen mind. (Such a response from a counselor seems unimaginable now, when school officials are much more responsive to racist bullying.) We both knew that Michael was acting like a bigoted bully, and we both knew that wasn't grounds enough to get him into any trouble. I would need to keep biting my tongue. Ignore the slurs spat in my face and absorb the smaller slights that cut. This is what it meant to be a Muslim Pakistani American girl growing up in America.

"You have to learn to deal with it."

No one was going to save me from indignity. No one was going to stand up for me when I was wronged. No one was going to call out Michael, the coach who taught health, or the popular white girl looking for ways to embarrass me. No one would tell them to do better. They were teaching me how to navigate white America's regular slights and insults, which were as likely to come from the educated, white upper middle class as the stereotypical crass and ignorant bigots. These were lessons that would serve me for years to come. I never told anyone about my conversation with Mr. Smith. I went back to ignoring Michael's name-calling in the pickup lot.

It took decades to loosen the grip of those lessons.

I was thirty-two when I spoke about Michael publicly for the first time. The St. Louis Press Club invited me to speak on a panel about the media's role in addressing prejudice in society. I was working as a newspaper reporter at the *St. Louis Post-Dispatch*, where I had landed after graduate school in Chicago. I told the audience about how Michael had treated me in seventh grade, how my counselor had responded, and how I had followed his advice.

"I don't really get stung by slurs," I said back then. "Those are slingshots of the ignorant."

I discovered that calling out bullies and the adults who enable them could be empowering even decades later.

Around this time, I had joined Facebook and reconnected with childhood friends and a few frenemies from those middle-school days, including Michael. (In high school, Michael ended up dating one of my friends, so we occasionally interacted. We never really talked about seventh grade.) I sent him a private message, reminding him what he used to call my mom and how it had made me feel that year.

He never responded and defriended me.

I could tell from his posts and photos that he served in the military sometime after graduating. I saw photos he posted of himself stationed in the Middle East. I wondered if he called anyone a raghead while he was there.

Maybe he had evolved from his middle-school self as much as I have.

Of course, there will be some people who won't like me for who I am.

I'm finding my own way to "deal with it," Mr. Smith.

Untitled

by Trung Le Nguyen

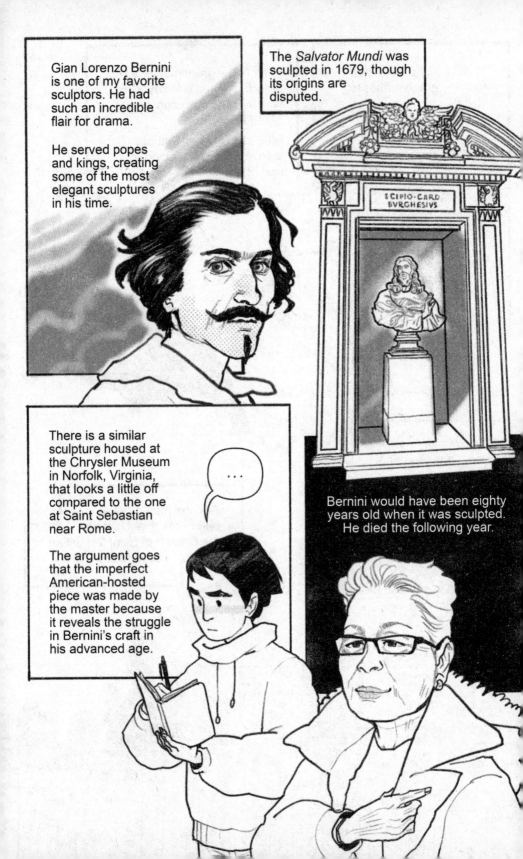

His work is all over Rome,
and I so badly wanted to tell
my grandmother all about him.

I wanted her to know that
in life he was a huge cad,
jealous and vindictive,
who was formally exonerated
for his crimes and sins
by the pope himself.

I wanted to describe his
magnificent technique
and his impact on me
and the world.

But my language skills
just weren't strong
enough.

It would be like
trying to replicate
a Bernini on paper
with a ballpoint pen.

Things Better Left Unsaid

by Dương Nguyễn Ca Dao

I don't intend for my story to be some remarkable revelation about the Vietnamese American identity or a tale of racial justice served with a clear beginning, middle, and end. It is simply a story of human error—my human error—one that I believe other young Viets might see themselves in . . . and, I hope, forgive themselves for.

I became more involved in the activist space during the summer of 2020, joining in Black Lives Matter protests, digesting history lessons that my schools had chosen to ignore, and internalizing the lexicon of social justice. Following in the footsteps of Asian American activists, I would do my due diligence on social media, expressing outrage at the stereotype of the good, quiet, acquiescent Asian within Western literature or putting out content aimed at redefining the Asian American experience. But in my heart, I knew that I had once been the embodiment of what I now scorn publicly. For years, I had lived by the mantra *Make yourself small enough that people will sometimes forget you are even there. Don't speak up—nobody's listening anyway. Don't humiliate yourself. Save face.*

By the time I was a high school freshman, I had successfully negotiated these terms and conditions with myself, trade-offs I deemed worth a shot at existing as a foreigner in this so-called land of opportunity.

I was wrong.

It was 2012, and Michael Kors and its luxury handbags had swept malls across America. My mom fell in love with those bags. And for the first time, this sort of material indulgence was within reach, thanks to the discounts department stores like Macy's offered. Most weekends, we would head to the mall to browse the sales and drop by affordable shops like Forever 21. We'd leave happily with a bargain or two in hand. Our ventures into designer stores were few and far between, and often my idea. Like many kids who lived with few material possessions, I was dazzled by designer goods and loved to pretend that we could pass off as regulars at these shops, perusing the thousand-dollar items on display and leaving empty-handed *only* because nothing was satisfactory enough to purchase.

But that July weekend, it was my mom who decided to stop by the brick-and-mortar Michael Kors store, where they sold higher-end pieces that were definitely out of our budget. Delighted by this turn of events and grateful for the extra time out of the sweltering Oklahoma heat, I made a beeline toward the white marbled entrance, my mother in tow.

Shelves of beautiful leather bags lined the walls. The black wooden floors gleamed under glass cases that showed off an abundance of watches and luxury trinkets. We were among a few customers occupying the brightly lit space, along with three white, tall, slim associates dressed all in black. I smiled awkwardly at them, suddenly feeling exposed by the harsh lights. The three women smiled back, but it didn't reach their eyes. My mom and I had entered enough commercial spaces to expect a sales pitch as soon as we walked in or, at the very least, a casual chat about the weather. But none of the three women spoke to us. I moved closer to Mom as she glided to the wall to inspect each bag, a smile fixed on her face. We huddled together, our backs to the store associates who remained mute and watchful. As I brushed my fingers over the clasps and locks of each purse, my mind was racing to find a way to fill the silence that was expanding behind us.

I did not know how to interact with the store associates, and I quickly gathered that they had little interest in interacting with "customers" like us: an Asian woman who did not speak English well and her teenage kid who clearly wasn't in charge of the credit cards. These well-dressed, shiny-haired women took one look at my mom's checkered Bermuda shorts and faded T-shirt and decided that she was going to be the subject of their subtle ridicule, of dirty looks I caught in the mirror.

As I looked around the store, I saw the way the other customers were scrutinizing us too: young white women sneering at my mother as she accessorized her round, tanned shoulders with the fancy handbags, as she happily admired herself in front of the mirror in the middle of the store, perhaps willfully unaware of the silence emanating from the store associates who stood like stony statues behind her. And in that small eternity of humiliation, I began to feel a quiet hatred toward my mom. How dare she decide to invade a space that was never meant for us? Can she not see how different we are from the store's clientele? Does she not see how dark and out of place we look?

So, I did something that haunts me to this day: I let out a laugh at my mother's expense, one that was meant to put me on the same side as the store associates. Then I made a show out of concealing the laughter so the women would notice. It was like I was trying to say, *See? I, too, think my mom looks ridiculous. But don't worry; I'm not like her.* For the first time in my life, I wanted so badly to distance myself from my mother's unquestionably Other identity because I could not bear the judgment coming from these women. Because it confirmed everything I had feared about my hyphenated identity: that I was lesser than the people who, for all intents and purposes, owned this country. I was ashamed of my mom for all the ways that she was different from America. And by extension, I hated myself too.

"Mhm? You don't like this bag?" my mom asked in Vietnamese when she saw me covering my laugh.

"No, it's ugly," I replied, wishing that she would put it down and stop embarrassing us both.

"You should try this bag here!" One of the sales associates finally deigned to speak to us, offering my mom a purse I knew she wouldn't like.

"Thank you," Mom said anyway, and tried it on, perhaps to not upset the girl. How ironic that, in our own ways, we were both trying to please the people whose job it was to help us. Now it was my turn to stand immobile, ashamed and angry and confused about my own reaction. Mom saw my body language and finally put the bag down. We walked out of there, her hand empty of a new purse and my heart full of regret. We didn't talk about what happened at all.

I've wrestled with making sense of this interaction for years. Why did I not say anything to those racist salespeople? Why did I turn my back on my own mother when she was at her most vulnerable? I have tried to nonchalantly bring up the encounter with her a few times over the years. The language barrier paired with my reticence to discuss my shameful behavior have made it nearly impossible to really unpack the moment. One time, I expressed to her that I thought it wasn't right that the sales associates had treated her like dirt. She had responded with a resigned shrug, as if to say, *It is what it is.* We were foreigners and had no right to make demands. This from a woman whom I had once been deathly afraid of, a woman who never would have accepted that kind of treatment from a Vietnamese-speaking merchant. But she had internalized that she was "less than" these women. I had done the same.

As I write these words, I catch myself questioning whether I have blown all of it out of proportion, that perhaps this story is not worth memorializing. Surely, I have experienced other, more dramatic examples of racism in my life. And yet this is the memory I always return to. I've learned that my racial identity in America has been shaped not by made-for-movie confrontations, with me as a helpless victim facing off with a haughty aggressor. No, it has been moments like these, when the attacks have been less overt and the emotions have been more complicated. I had rationalized hurting my own mother for the mere possibility of fitting in. And I would go on to hurt my parents many more times in my effort to leave behind traces of myself that didn't belong in the dominant culture. Throughout my teenage years, I erased so much of myself that I lost track of who I was.

When I moved to California for college, the emotions associated with this memory evolved. Being out of the house and away from my mom allowed me to see things differently. She and I did not always have an easy relationship. Still, I knew how much she loved me, even if she showed her love in ways I didn't always understand. The way my mind continually conjured this painful memory was somehow a clear testament to the deep love I had for her, this fiery and resilient woman whom I feared, resented, was in awe of, and *thương* with all of my heart. And with that realization, I was on a journey to pick up the pieces of myself that I had discarded . . . a journey of healing.

As of this writing, I am twenty-three and the president of a not-for-profit Vietnamese-language newsroom, whose mission is to translate verifiable news into Vietnamese to eliminate the language barrier and thereby amplify the political voice of the Vietnamese American community. Not bad for a girl who used to hate that part of herself. I suspect that there is a straight line connecting this memory with where I stand today within the diaspora. Giving Viet voices a platform was something I wish I could have done for my mother on that terrible day. I wish I could have been her translator and protector. I wish I would have told those workers that they needed to go fuck themselves. I hope that she can one day forgive me for the transgression in my heart.

As an Asian American, I have grown up feeling like so many of my emotions were wrong and that I could not afford to make mistakes. I hope my incredibly flawed story relieves many of that guilt that no child should have to bear. My loneliness, my fears, my missteps, and, eventually, my little triumphs are as valid as my hyphenated identity. I hope every immigrant and their children know that they do not need to make themselves small for anyone, because they themselves are enough—*more* than enough.

How Do I Begin to Speak of Your Perfection?

A LOVE POEM FOR ASIAN AMERICANS

by Sokunthary Svay

Your beauty triggers them.

It is the very nature of you.

Freckled   porcelain
Blemished   sun-kissed
Moon-shaped heart-like

It's the eyes. They always give you away.

Folds
Slant
Cursive   They cry all the same.

. . .

My daughter describes her migraine auras
As a DNA strand.

. . .

I am the rice grown
In my father's hometown of Takeo.

I come from a language
That makes relatives out of strangers.

And yet my mother couldn't
Teach me in her Khmer words.
We have different heart languages.
That was the barrier,
That Mekong of a river to cross.

I am waving to her from one side
Unable to swim across. I'm trying
To find a boat, constructed of my own hands.

. . .

There are strangers who weaponize language
To disconnect from us.

But this poem is not for them.

. . .

I am older than the music instructor
Who ends class early because her mother just died.
I'm the last to leave.

I tell her a mother's truth:
My daughter's very existence fills me with pride.

That kind of love endures into the beyond
Of what expanses we can't reach.

When the body gives way, there are still remnants of us.

. . .

I find joy in relearning my heritage language.
To say "like" in Khmer is ចូលចិត្ត
Literally to "enter the heart."

. . .

When I see you, I sing.

There is value in choosing how to be seen, in reclaiming the right to select the face you show the world, in insisting that others see you as you know yourself to be. In proudly and boldly framing ourselves in the ways of our own choosing, to say: *Here I am, this is me.*

—CELESTE NG

On Being Black and Asian in America

by Kimiko Matsuda-Lawrence

Checking the Box

First grade. I am six years old, taking my first standardized test at Shepherd Elementary School in Washington, DC. Next to "Race," I check "Black." At six, I already know what they think about me. What they think about us. I see the white schools when we drive across Rock Creek Park to play against them in basketball—with their sparkling hallways, their fancy, shiny gyms with the school mascot printed on the half-court line, smiling up at us, taunting us, making us feel small.

At our school on the Black side of the Park, we play basketball in the tiny auditorium, with duct tape on the floor for lines, plastic hoops wheeled in from the basement, and a ceiling so low you can't even shoot a three-pointer without a chunk of the ceiling falling down on you. Our parents have to show up and yell at the school board for basic things: to get AC or heat in the classrooms, to stop the slime oozing down the classroom walls. We have to fundraise for supplies for the teachers, for musical instruments, for new uniforms, for new anything.

This is the same year my class wins the "I Love Life" song competition—a citywide competition created because Black kids in DC—kids our age—are already planning their funerals, designing tribute T-shirts, not expecting to live long enough to grow up in a city that is trying to kill them. We practice which forks to use for the fancy awards banquet, we get dressed up, we stand up on that stage in our Sunday best, we sing with all our hearts: "I love life, I want to live!"

At six years old, I already know what they expect of me. I know the future they have written for me. I see how the world thinks of us, how they treat us—what they give us versus what they give them. Who they prioritize, who they forget. I see the lines drawn around my life, the lines carved through my city, the lines going back centuries that shape my world, that tell me I am not smart, I am not valued, I do not matter.

But I know these lines are not mine, were never mine. And despite everything the world tells me about myself every single day, at six years old, I know that I am smart.

So, I pick up my number-two pencil, and I check "Black." To prove them wrong.

Why

Second grade. I am seven years old. My mom comes in to tell my class about being Japanese. She bakes butter mochi, teaches us origami, passes around the *Rafu Shimpo*. As my classmates flip through the newspaper, a photo catches their eye. I look at what my classmates are pointing at: caricatured Asian faces, slanted eyes, words in fake Asian font: *Wong Brothers Laundry—Two Wongs can make it white* emblazoned on Abercrombie & Fitch T-shirts.

My mom tells us Asian people face racism, just like Black people. She points at the pictures, asks us, *Does that look like me? No*, my class says, shaking their heads.

I stare at the Asian faces on those shirts. They look nothing like my mom; they look nothing like me. I am the only Asian kid in my class, and sometimes I hear my classmates make ching chong Chinaman talk, or see them pull their eyes like that, or call our volunteer chess teacher Mr. Tsunami when his name is actually Minami, or make fun of the "smelly" musubi my mom packs in my lunch. I stare at those Abercrombie shirts, and it makes me feel the same way I feel when my classmates do that stuff: like something is wrong with me, like something is wrong with my mom. And lonely, real lonely, like I want to go hide, like I want to disappear.

When my mom is done, she asks if we have any questions.

My classmate Stephen raises his hand. *Ms. Matsuda, why do white people hate us so much?*

A classroom full of Black second graders stares back at my Asian mom, waiting for an answer, as my mom searches for words.

We are young, but we already know.

The First Time

Seventh grade. I am thirteen years old. Riding the chartered city bus that carries us Black kids across the Park to our middle school on the white side of the city. On the way to school, this drunk white man gets on the bus, belligerent, angry, yelling. He calls us all the N-word, tells us we're all going to hell. The boys at the back of the bus stand up, pushing forward, ready to fight. I am hot, I am shaking, my heart is pounding. I see the hate in his eyes, the way he looks at us, like we're animals.

The bus driver manages to kick him off, and we ride the rest of the way to school in silence. We walk through the cops and metal detectors at the entrance. We eat lunch in the cafeteria, where the Black kids sit on one side of the pillars, and the white kids on the other. We sit in fourth-period Algebra 1, where there are only four of us, where the white kids who walk to school instead of riding a bus make fun of our names and call us ghetto when they think we're not listening, where we are always trying to prove them wrong.

That day, I go home and tell my mom about the white man on the bus. I sit there in the kitchen while she calls the city bus company and reports the incident, getting more and more worked up. I look at my mom. She is angry. She is hurt. But that man on the bus, he was talking to me. He was calling *me* that. Not her. She is hurt, but she is not hurting like I am. Sitting there in the kitchen, suddenly, I feel the gap between us. The ways in which she is safe and I am not. And I realize, she cannot protect me. I sit there in the kitchen, with the weight of all this. I am still shaking.

Mirror

Freshman year of high school. I am fourteen years old. We have just moved to Honolulu, where my mom is from, where I'm one of two half-Black kids in my class. Pretty much everyone else is Asian or Pacific Islander, and even though I'm half-Asian, I feel so different here. My classmates hang out in cliques: the Japanese, the Filipinos, the Polynesians. I don't know where I fit in. The girls in my class comment on my butt, tell me my body reminds them of Nicki Minaj. I know it's a compliment, but it feels weird. I miss Black people.

One day, this Asian kid in my class comes to school wearing a T-shirt covered in cartoon animals wearing chains and grills, riding in a lowrider, eating fried chicken. When I see him at the lockers that morning wearing the shirt, my stomach drops. I stare at the T-shirt, at the twisted reflection staring back at me . . . and I know that shirt is talking about me. About us. This is what they think of us. This is how they see us. Like that white man on the bus. Like we're animals.

I want to tear that shirt right off him and rip it to shreds. I want to scream. But I don't say anything. I just walk right by, try not to look at him in class, avert my eyes when we pass by in the hallway, look at the floor when I see him in the cafeteria.

I steal glances at the other half-Black kid in my class. I wonder if he sees the shirt, if it hurts him like it hurts me. I want to ask him, I want to reach out, but I can't find the words. We move around each other silently in the tiny world of our school, an invisible line tying us to each other, holding the same weight. But we never talk about the shirt, never talk about how lonely we are. How much we need each other.

The kid in my class wears the shirt to school again. And again. And again. Every time he wears it, I don't know what to do. I think about what I'd say, plan it all out in my head. A couple times, I almost say something. But when I see him at the lockers in the morning the next time he wears it, I can't do it—I just pass by like nothing's wrong. Every time, I hate myself for not saying anything. I feel like my silence is permission, like my silence somehow makes it okay for him to wear that shirt. Like this is my fault.

He keeps wearing the shirt. I never say anything.

Just a Word

Senior year. I am eighteen years old. There's this kid in my class who won't stop saying the N-word. One day, I can't hold it in anymore—something breaks open inside me, and I go off on him. I tell him about the history of that word, tell him how much it hurts me.

You can't say that, I say.

It's just a word, he keeps saying.

It's just a word.

It's just a word.

He never apologizes.

The night of graduation, we do a senior class lock-in at a hotel in Waikiki. We're locked in this big banquet hall, and they make us do this exercise where we go around in a circle and hug every person in our class. I'm dreading getting to him. I don't want to hug him, I don't want him to touch me. Then he's in front of me, going in for the hug, then his arms are around me, and all of a sudden I'm sobbing, I'm shaking, it's all coming out, and it feels like a dream and a nightmare, and then it's over.

Ten years later, I still have dreams about it, I still wake up shaking.

Welcome

My first week at Harvard, the Asian American Association shows up at my dorm room. They look down at their list, then back up at my face, confused.

Is your roommate home? they say, scanning the room behind me. *We're looking for Kimiko.*

I am Kimiko, I say.

Oh, they say. They stare at me. At my brown face, my curly hair, unable to process.

I take their invitation; I close the door. I never show up to a meeting.

Choice

One month later, an anti–affirmative action op-ed published in the *Harvard Crimson* blows up on campus. Suddenly, everywhere we go, people are talking about us—in the dining hall, in the dorms, in classrooms and lecture halls—debating whether we deserve to be here, saying we got in just because we're Black. My Black classmates are talking about their SAT scores and AP classes, trying to defend our presence on this campus, trying to fight off the sickening feeling that we aren't wanted here.

Back in my dorm room, I am the only one. At the beginning of the year, before the affirmative action article blew up, I'd hang out with my three Asian roommates a lot. But now I take shelter in the Black community on campus, sit at the Black table in the dining hall, where I know everyone is feeling the exact same way I'm feeling right now. We are under attack, and this is the only place I feel safe. I worry that my Asian roommates are talking about me too, saying the same things as the white kids when I'm not around, agreeing with that article that said I shouldn't be here. I know everyone on campus thinks *they* deserve to be here, never questions whether *they* got in on merit. There's an unspoken assumption on campus: their faces belong here, mine does not. And nothing—not my Japanese name, or my SAT scores, or my grades—will change that.

This is the moment I realize: Yeah, I'm half-Asian—but when Black people are attacked, my Asianness doesn't protect me. I can't hide. I can't choose. In this moment, I am Black.

Betrayal

I'm in my first job, sitting in the back of the car, on the way to the Women's March. My white woman boss, who is sitting next to me, casually drops the N-word. My other boss, a half-Asian, half-white woman, doesn't say anything. No one says anything, and the conversation moves on. I sit there shaking, but no one sees. I want to say something, I want to scream, but my voice is gone. At the next truck stop, I lock myself in a bathroom stall and cry. I don't want to get back in that car.

A couple years later, I'm in another job, sitting in a room full of Black people. Someone says a joke, and the word hits me. *Jap*. They called my grandpa that when they locked his family up behind barbed wire at Heart Mountain during World War II. My cousin's high-school baseball coach called him that a few years ago, and he quit baseball.

No one says anything, and the conversation moves on. I sit there shaking, but no one sees. I want to say something, I want to scream, but my voice is gone.

Safety

You wish you could pitch your body into the space of the
    nonnegotiable
This is the body that says *NO*
I will not move
I will not bend my rules

I will not let this happen
But you are swallowing your scream again
And suddenly you are the person
Who has made it okay to say this
Who has made this an okay thing to say
But it is not okay
And your body knows this
But it is too busy negotiating its presence
So that you can stay here

Progress

2021. I am twenty-seven years old. I'm sitting in the living room, surrounded by Black people. The news is playing. On the television, Biden is signing a bill, surrounded by smiling Asian people. But the people in this living room aren't smiling. They're saying, *They got it so fast.* They're saying, *We can't even get an anti-lynching bill.*

The underlying sentiment: *they'll never do that for us.*

I feel so much at once. I know about Vincent Chin. I know about the Chinese massacres in the late 1800s. I know about my cousin who was attacked on the street in New York last year in the wave of anti-Asian hate crimes during COVID.

I know all this and yet—

They got it so fast.

I also know fast is relative. Because everything is slow for us. Because it's been four hundred years, and we are still waiting, always waiting—for a country that will never protect us.

I look at the Asian people on the TV, smiling and cheering. But sitting here in this room full of Black people, in the body that I live in, I don't feel like part of it. I feel guilty, both for not feeling fully able to join in the celebration of this moment that should be my right as an Asian American—and for getting something that everyone else in this room has yet to have.

Because I'm also feeling what everyone else in this room is feeling. The pain of being forgotten, the betrayal of always being last, the knowledge that America will never pass a hate crime law for us. Because America itself is committing the hate crimes; America itself is killing us.

Then, on the news, they play leaked footage of cops beating a Black man to death in Louisiana.

I stare down at the floor. I can't watch.

I don't feel like celebrating.

What Are You?

I'm Japanese

I go to Bon dances every summer, I know how to cook all the New Year's foods, I eat natto, I wash my rice until the water runs clear, I take my shoes off at the door, I never show up without omiyage, I never take the last piece, I hold back, I apologize constantly, I say *no no no* when I want to say yes, I say *yes* when I should probably say no

I'm Black

I walk into a store

                  and no one greets me

I walk into a restaurant

                      and no one serves me

I walk into a neighborhood

                            and everyone stares

Sides

Sometimes
There is a line, and I know which side of it I fall on
It's never straight down the middle
I'm never *just* an Asian girl

Yes, I am Asian, but I will always be Black.

An Incomplete Silence

by Kim Tran

My mother is an extremely talkative woman. I joke that she is the mayor of the neighborhood. I know about almost every family on our block, because she tells me about dropping off plates of chow mein at their nearby houses. You can often catch her chatting over the fence in our backyard about someone's kid's job (or lack thereof). She is the type of woman who will talk your ear off at the supermarket. Do you need someone to do some landscaping on your yard? My mom knows the perfect person for the job . . . *and* he'll cut you a deal. Having trouble with your car? Her nephew is a mechanic. Don't worry— he's nearby. She's full of good tips, guidance, and advice. She gives it freely, often, and loudly.

A similar cacophony existed inside the homes in which I was raised. When I was growing up, twenty-five of my family members lived off of one main street. We gathered weekly at my aunt's home, where small pods of cousins would collect around the house and in the backyard. Our older members would sit at the kitchen table with the women who raised them, drinking jasmine tea, gossiping, and eating Costco pastries. My cohort of cousins would play a game we created upstairs. Sometimes we pretended to be in a grocery store, mimicking the price-conscious buying habits of our parents. Other times, we solemnly acted out the Catholic mass services we attended on Sundays, employing tamarind candies as communion wafers.

For the entirety of my childhood and for much of my young adulthood, I was *never* alone. It was *never* quiet. Secrets were *never* private. If someone asked me then what it meant to be Vietnamese, I would have described this gregarious and sometimes-overwhelming auditory experience of weekend afternoons.

All of that changed when I came out.

The first time I kissed a girl I wrote it off. I thought that I was too Catholic, too confused, and too drunk to know any better. The second time, I told myself I had done it for attention. The third time was different. It merited introspection, fear, and disclosure. Driving home from a Sunday church service, spurred by optimism and shielded by the veil of indirect eye contact, I made a spontaneous decision. I told my mother that when I finally brought someone home to meet the family it might not be a cisgender man. To my utter horror, my big reveal was met with total and absolute silence.

In the fourteen years since that car ride, my mother has met many milestones with this same response. She cried wordlessly when I told her I had been in a queer relationship for a year. She refused to acknowledge me when I corrected her misgendering my partner. She simply did not attend a public talk I gave on queer and trans inclusion, even though it was only an hour from her house. She did not react when, five years after I met my partner, I told her that I had gotten engaged. With a few key exceptions, the rest of my family followed suit.

Coming out has been a lesson in silence. It characterizes my uneasy existence at the intersection of two realities: membership to a Vietnamese family that struggles with my sexuality and to a queer community who can't fully understand what it means to live in my culture. Silence is what I hear when I cannot fully be myself.

The absence of noise is instructive and dynamic. It is a cue, marker, and model all in one. Silence tells us what we can or cannot discuss; it often intimates that shame is the reason why.

Consider walking into a room full of people talking when all of a sudden the chatter and all movement cease. The abrupt about-face communicates a myriad of responses: discomfort, embarrassment, awkwardness, and, most importantly, pain for its bearer. Silence, then, is not an auditory experience, but a social one. It is why cousins only say nefarious things when I am out of earshot or not in attendance. It is why aunties mention my absence but not its obvious reason. Silence is why their rolled eyes and glares are as soundless as they are painful. Yet, imposed silence doesn't change the fact that people like me with voices like mine are growing in number.

Millennials are twice as likely as previous generations to be a part of the queer and trans community. A recent Gallup poll finds that the sharpest increases in our numbers are among Asian and Latinx people. To wit, I am and have always been surrounded by queer and trans people of color. Many of my friends and colleagues, along with my first girlfriend and my current partner, are both queer and Asian. I feel loved because I *am* loved by people who see me through the lens of shared experience. However, this reality can do little to challenge our exclusion from our families of origin. It has minimal impact on whether or not unspoken judgment or intolerance continues to shape our lives.

When I came out, my mother taught me that silence is defined by absence: the absence of comfort, acceptance, and, most of all, power. I still experience many of these things when it comes to my family. There are whisper campaigns and unstated disapproval, but I am learning that silence is as fragile as it is overwhelming and that neither is absolute or permanent.

I had two Sunday-school teachers: Mateo and Adrian. They had soft smiles and easy demeanors. (Mateo always saved me blue crayons because they were my favorite. In turn, he was my favorite instructor.) I came close to enjoying their classes about a religion I would ultimately leave. After every class, they departed together, in the same sedan. My mother told me that they were roommates. One day, Mateo and Adrian stopped coming to the carpeted room where I spent weekends coloring in scenes from the Bible. After they were gone, I overheard a conversation between my mother and another parishioner. My mother was the first to say that the church had made a mistake, that it wasn't right that Mateo and Adrian couldn't teach anymore, that it didn't matter what their "lifestyle" might be. My mother never told me why or how they left. I never brought it up. I simply knew that for my mother, queerness did not justify exile.

Silence is porous. Many things can break through its seeming totality. Absence is never as all-encompassing as it seems.

Five years ago, I introduced my partner to my mother. We went to a fancy Vietnamese restaurant in San Francisco. Everyone wanted to make a good first impression. There is a picture of the three of us from that day. I am holding my phone at arm's length, trying to find the best angle. It is slightly blurry because my hands are wobbling from laughing at a joke my partner is telling my mom. My mother is whispering in my ear about how she needs to fix her hair. The restaurant is crowded behind us. It feels like there are a million people talking. We struggle to hear each other over all the noise.

Ten Things You Should Know about Being an Asian from the South

by G Yamazawa

1

Between fried chicken and teriyaki chicken, "What's your favorite
food?"
will become a very difficult question to answer.

2

When you smile, they'll ridicule your eyes
for being smaller than usual.
Remind yourself, it's only because America
always wants to be able
to see through you.

3

When you forget where you're from
you'll truly become
American.

4

When they speak of Black folk and White folk
do not simply take sides.
A wolf will become friends with a sheep
as long as its kindness leads to something
it can dig its teeth into.

5

They'll try to call you all kinds of things like
Bruce Lee, Jet Li, Jackie Chan, Kristi Yamaguchi,
and Hong Kong Phooey.
Laugh at their ignorance, it will give you strength.
Remind yourself
when you were a boy,
being deemed as powerful of a man as Bruce Lee
still made you feel weak
and helpless.

6

I never really liked list poems like this
but I figured it'd be fitting
since Asians are supposed to be good with numbers.

7

Don't get mad at innocent ignorance 'cause some shit
is just funny.
One day a classmate asked me what I was.
When I told her I was Japanese, she said,
"Ohhhhhhhhh, I thought you was Asian!"

8

When they call you Chinese
correct them.

9

Upon correcting them, tell them your full name
in your native dialect.
Remind them of your parents' birthplace.
Remind them of Hiroshima and Nagasaki
until the conversation feels nuclear.
Remind them of your ancestors who danced
with swords until their choreography was lethal.
Remind yourself you are only reminding yourself

because after the entire conversation
you'll still be Chinese
to them.

10
Find time to search inside
a smile won't shine
unless you wear it with pride
every time I would laugh
I would cover my eyes
I now realize I have nothing to hide
I like my chicken
teriyaki or fried
I like my fried rice
wit hot sauce on the side

but there were plenty things
I had to sacrifice too
I used to sell half pounds
to half of my school
but I got my own flow
I won't rap like you
cuz dawg, I'm Asian

I eat cats like you.

Unzipping

by Riss M. Neilson

I am thirty-three.

My oldest child sits on the floor while I weave cornrows into her hair. The bones in my fingers feel overworked. She is tender headed. We both complain, but we are happy with our time together. *I like it out in a bush just fine*, she says. Her friends call it a bush, but she doesn't care; she laughs, she lets it keep reaching for the sun until wash day. In this moment, she is a copy of me. It's how I like mine too, but I am defensive of her because kids teased me in middle school until my momma sent me to the salon for straight hair. *It's a beautiful bush*, I tell her. *You are a green, growing thing, like me.* Our hair is thick and unruly, matted in the middle, and we both prefer it wild. My email goes off while she's handing me a black rubber band. She wonders what I'm reading. I wonder what I'm reading.

I am asked to write for this anthology, about growing up as an Asian in America, but I'm not sure the email belongs to me. I don't finish my daughter's braids. She is happy when I kiss the top of her head, start unwinding what has been done. She stands and shakes her hair out, runs off to play or paint or draw with her sister. I am excited about the offer but double-check to make sure it's mine to keep. I don't know yet that someone I admire will say, *Is Riss even Asian?* And I'll spend too much time wondering if I'm Asian enough to write about it. I don't know yet that it is exactly these words, this wondering, that makes writing about it feel necessary. That I will feel propelled to look at my children, who can check one more race box than I can, and wonder if they will ever be asked to write or make art related to their experiences. Maybe they'll consider if and where and how much they belong in those spaces too. I don't know yet that this essay will be a coil of alternating things, which cause me to realize I am not only questioning but quieting the mixed parts of me while writing it. On some real meta shit, I will go all the way in, not talking about the whole of *me* while attempting to write an essay on *my* Asian experience (a mixed person's experience). I will laugh at how messy my subconscious is. But I don't know it yet. What I do know is, I will reread the email to feel joy.

I am months younger and can finally afford to fix a chipped tooth. But I need my mom's firmness to prep me for the pain of the complimentary cleaning. The hygienist calls me in the room, points her chin at the chair for me to *sit, sit.* I don't want to be presumptuous, but her accent has me sitting with the quickness, snapping me back to childhood commands. She squints at me before starting. *What is your nationality?* A spark of joy goes through me because I think she sees a connection. *I'm part Filipina. Are you Filipina, too?* She smiles, says she is, but her eyes fix on my Afro. *Why is your hair so big?* Years ago, I may have wanted to shrink, to fish for an elastic and make myself smaller to fit her chair just right, but I let myself take up space. I tell her it's from my Cape Verdean side, and we talk about my West African ancestry briefly before talking adobo and possible visits to the Philippines. When she types my answers into the computer, I realize she asked questions about my race and nationality because she was required to. Still, I appreciate the way she speaks to me of Manila and Zamboanga while opening my mouth wide and glancing at all of my childhood silvers. I decide when she starts scraping, hitting those sensitive spots near my gums, I'll trust her to do it. She must trust me, too, because when I don't follow directions well she raises her voice—the frustrated, short-tempered familiarity that has me remembering my grandfather. Anyone else might complain about her, but right now she feels like family. And family tells me I need to learn to bite down. *Do it right.*

I am already pandemic-tired when the news hits.

There are loose directions to follow: voice opinions, donate, repost. I do all of this, but mostly I cry, bawl at seeing and hearing about the attacks on the grandmothers, the aunties, the grand-fathers. My own lolo is in the Philippines. *Papa, just checking on you?* I receive pictures of him watering plants he has grown before his wife FaceTimes me. They're eating breakfast. *Guava from our tree,* Papa says, and points to the fruits he collected. It's been too long since I've seen his face, technology offering something like a hug in a moment of wishing I could wrap my arms around him. I wonder if he feels it too. Suddenly, I am eight, and Papa and I are two strands wound together while walking blocks in Silver Lake, buying penny candies from the corner store before cavities exist. I jump over cracks so I don't break my momma's back and Papa smacks the back of my head. *Pay attention or you'll fall, goddammit.* I am always scraped knees and bruises and he yells when he's worried but lags behind to watch my step. I blink back to now, tell myself he's safe where he is, while news of the attacks hit social media in a wave and the undercurrents rip through me, through so many. *Are you coming back to the States soon?* I ask. He doesn't mention the attacks; I'm not sure he knows. If he did, he'd laugh, say if someone tries him, he'll *beat ass.* He's always been a badass, my lolo. But he's got gout now, bad knees, and high blood pressure. I'm the one who'd have to watch his step, be his backbone. He says it'll be a few months till he comes back and I wonder if he should just stay where he is. I used to think this was his home, but maybe the Philippines gives him the kind of home America can't. When we hang up, the sky is dark and I am a mess of dark things.

I want my aunties strapped with shanks and pepper spray. My mom works as a phlebotomist, and a white man waiting for his bloodwork threatened an Asian man who had a small child with him—*You brought COVID to us, you're dirty, go back to your country.* Mom says the guards handled it, trying to calm me though she has a shake in her voice. My mind runs wild. It produces a sequence of events where the guards can't protect her when she's working alone in a room with so many sharps. She is a small woman; she uses needles to draw blood of men four times her size who fuss about the pain. The blood of people who are like that white man. *If anyone ever tries to touch you, if anyone hurts you, stab them in the eye with a needle,* I tell her. *Riss,* she hisses, *I'll be fine.* But I can't protect her when she's away from me. She tells me she's my mom, says she's the one who needs to protect me. But we aren't an exact replication. I am less Asian than she is. In this place I call home, sometimes not Asian at all.

I am adult-ish.

Tumbling through my late teens and into messier twenties with friends as we lie out on dorm beds to spiral about sex without protection. About good sex and bad sex, how many people we've done it with, stupid shit like stinky balls and unwashed ass. We dip into dreaming of vacations that are far from my broke reach; we laugh about marriage, *nah, never.* Then we bullshit, *nah, never,* about having future babies too. One friend has earth-toned skin and society got us fucked up because she hopes her babies end up with *the good hair.* Another says she only dates within her Hispanic culture and her kids will be Hispanic too, that's on that. I joke that if her kids could inherit both chromosome copies from her, she would want them to. We're high as shit and laughing, but I stop when they wonder what my kids will look like. *They bout to be some mixed ass babies. How do you want them to look?* I don't know what to say. I don't know yet that mixed babies are fetishized. All I know is my roots are too many and reach places I'll probably never see. I like all kinds of guys; I like girls too. But then I start dreaming of babies who look like me and when the THC doubles back they are three-dimensional beings.

I am a teenager.

Walking to catch the bus from high school in the summer is a pattern made up of sweating out the smell of weed, saying fuck the crosswalk to risk getting run over, stopping at the clothing stores, grabbing slices of pizza, and flirting with other kids from different schools.

Kennedy Plaza bus station is gray, but the people in it are many shades and their auras fill the space with rainbow light. Yellow, blue, green, and red float above me as we wait for the buses. The boys say nasty shit; my home girls and I laugh: *Shut up, stop playing, word?* But when the boys start listing off favorite positions, naming girls who give the best head, the ones who give the worst, when they turn my way and say, *Bet Riss got that wet. You know what they say about Filipino women,* I am not prepared. I don't know yet that I am not Asian until they are curious about the *villa in Manila,* until they want to dip their fingers inside of me and see how much my body will give. I am not Asian until there is a benefit for them, for how good the sex will be. I am young and ignorant; my cheeks burn. I laugh at this acknowledgment of my heritage, no matter how ridiculous the theory sounds, because it's rare that anyone in high school acknowledges my Asianness at all. *See, she definitely got that wet,* they say. I don't know yet these things will still be said to me in my twenties and thirties. I am just hungry to be something at sixteen, accepted by one of the races I can check off. Not realizing what it means when those boys lick their lips and catalogue my pussy as a part they believe they can link to my Filipino ancestry. I don't know yet about the history of violence, of colonizers ravaging villages, that the *villa in Manila* is said to come from pain and rape. I am a mixed breed, alternating between one box and two more, trying not to mark "Other" for once. I won't know for years that I don't want to fit into a box if the only way I fit is by proving that yes, I got that wet. Yes, you want to find out. Yes, I'm Asian for you in this way, but not in the ways that count for me and my soul.

I am whatever a middle schooler is.

Scared to go to school. Scared of nicking my legs on a razor and of wearing a pad. Happy to fit in. These are some of the worst years, but my three best friends are Asian and so am I. They don't care that I can check a few boxes, that I usually check "Other" and can't speak another language. They bring me dumplings and I bring them lumpia. We rock corny matching shirts and we go to the bathroom together and we don't talk about being Asian because we just are. We walk home and boys follow, calling nasty shit out and running after us. One of my friends says something to them in Cambodian, then raises her middle finger in the air. I might not be able to speak another language, but I do know how to cuss a boy out in Tagalog because Papa taught me how. The boys who show up in the front of my house asking for me get a *putang ina mo*. Papa laughs when I say it. He tries teaching me more words, but I am busy worrying about shooting hoops with those same boys at the park, playing manhunt with my friends until the streetlights kick on. I don't retain any language other than the cusswords, but I know where the bugs hide, where to place my feet to climb trees, every Pokémon in the index, know how to treat a bee sting fast, know I have Papa for anything I need. But this is before the breakup that breaks our big-ass family into smaller parts. Before he and Nana separate and he marries a Filipina woman and moves with her to New York. Before I feel the loss of language like it's something that could've belonged to me too. Maybe I'd feel closer to Asian with Tagalog in my brain, my pocket, on paper—maybe I'd feel closer to him. I don't know yet that language will be a twisted ladder I can't climb. That I'll worry about the impending trip to the Philippines because I won't look or sound like I have roots there. I don't know yet that I won't have Creole, Italian, or Tagalog to pass on to my children, but what I will have is the cusswords. One day I'll *putang ina mo* any asshole who tries to mess with them.

I am two, four, eight, eleven.

Papa and I never talk about being Asian or what it means, but he throws parties with pancit and pork sinigang. I know the right amount of egg to make the lumpia wraps stick and how to fold and form them into the perfect three-dimensional shape. On weekdays, we make work of the yard. We plant in the garden and lie on grass he works hard to keep green. We get dirty; we take long winding walks through Providence, finding blooming flowers through breaks in the concrete, getting soft-serve ice cream and walking the hills of Neutaconkanut Park. We eat eggplant and grapes and ripened yellow pears from the yard. Papa teaches me about snakes, about the sun, about playing in the rain. He calls me Full Moon because of my round head. I am proud of my round head; I am Papa's full moon. He scares me with Filipino folklore, the ghost stories that coil in my mind right before bed. We fish every weekend; we clean them together. He tells me why blood is red, about death, and how to stop the pain for a stingray that gets accidentally caught on a hook. He lets me keep blue crabs I catch in a bucket. He tells me not to cry when they die. I cry and he yells that he told me not to cry. I tell him I'm a monster because I can't keep them alive. Then, he brings me to the Filipino market, shows me the blue crabs aren't reproductions but are cousins of the rock crabs we cook and eat all of the time.

I am a child, crouched low on the carpet with Papa.

He hands me a crab belly, shows me how he cracks it and cleans it out. I don't know yet that I will show this to my children, though I will wish it were him showing them. When it's my turn, he picks up another crab belly for himself and we are a mirror as he tells me, *Press down here. Do it right.* I do what I'm shown. He smiles. *Now we eat. Filipinos eat with our hands.*

And for a brief moment, I am a copy of him.

[It] is a part of the bitter undercurrent of Asian-American life that so many Asian graduates of elite universities find that meritocracy as they have understood it comes to an abrupt end after graduation.

—WESLEY YANG

The Question

by Mark Kramer

I can't remember the first time someone asked me the question "What are you?," but it happened early and often. From my barber. My Catholic after-school teacher. The deli guy. My friends' parents. The woman who, up to that point, I was actually excited to have matched with on Tinder. The radiologist making small talk while scanning my testicles for a tumor (balls were fine, dignity not so much). Hordes of semi-strangers with a curious eye and absolutely zero shame have asked me some version of the question "What are you?" There are tons of shorthand for it, whether it's the classic "Where are you from?," the defiant "Where are you *really* from?," the blunt "Where were you born?," the polite "Where are your parents from?," the not-so-subtle "Where's home?," and even the devious compliment "You look exotic." Perhaps because I've always been an ambiguous brown, as the son of a Jewish father from Brooklyn and a Filipino immigrant mother, "What are you?" is the version I remember best. Regardless, these are less actual questions and more piercing statements that give away what the not-so-private investigator is thinking: *You are not like me.*

Anytime I was with my father, "What are you?" became the racist elephant in the room. They'd look at him, then at me, back to him, then back to me, implying *what the hell is going on here?* as they rang up his Pall Malls. I must have heard it so many times that one of my earliest memories is my father telling me to answer the question by saying, "I'm American." Whatever the fuck that means. According to my observations, it was dry turkey and Lunchables and Hulk Hogan and a bald eagle eating a cheeseburger while shooting a machine gun at the moon and Indiana Jones (not Short Round) and skin as white as the Stars and Stripes. None of which were me.

Hearing those questions over and over was damaging to my developing psyche in two specific ways. First: from being identified as the Other, as the perpetual foreigner. *What is it about my face that makes you think it's okay to say that?* You realize you're different from everyone. And different feels unsafe. Especially for those born and raised in mostly white spaces, without an easily accessible community. I grew up on Staten Island, simultaneously known as the southern tip of New York City and the northern tip of the South. Its population consists of approximately eight Filipinos and one million Tony Soprano cosplayers. Between my mother the nurse and father the public-school teacher, we were lucky to have food on the table and go on the occasional family vacation. I don't remember much about those escapes, but I do remember being scared *all* the time. Besides my younger brother, I was different from literally everyone, including each of my parents. Different brought a lot of unwanted attention. Different meant my neighbor Vinny sprinted out of my birthday party at the sight of a mean-looking roasted lechon. Different meant that I came home from the bus every day with bruises up my arms courtesy of my "friends." It's not like my white side was doing me any favors either—a half-Italian and half-Jewish classmate was bullied because "there's no way they'd mix the best race with the worst one." (I'll let you guess which was which.) And as a Filipino who cannot sing or dance for shit, I've always felt like a fraud on my mom's side of the family. I last visited the Philippines as a third grader and can remember the terror that came from not speaking the language of anyone around me, from picking the ants out of my rice, showering with a bucket, and getting shoved around by the neighbor boy for, ironically, being American. I was the Other everywhere.

Second, "What are you?"—whether posed as innocent, insidious, or misguided small talk during a CT scan—led me to the only logical follow-up: *What am I?* That's a heavy question for any developing mind. It affected mine so much so, apparently, that a second-grade teacher told my parents I was "too serious" and "didn't know how to be a kid." That was wild for adult me to find out. Being a kid is one of the easiest jobs there is. Dedicated nap time? No meaningful decisions besides "Should I put this glue on paper or in my mouth?" Payment in the form of chicken nuggets? Sign me up! Childhood is supposed to be a time to gather valuable information about who you are, and who you want to be. You play a season of basketball, you suck, you learn you're the kind of person who sucks at basketball. You win your second-grade spelling bee, you learn you're good with words and think, *Hey, let's pull on that string.* The appropriate next step isn't to throw the third-grade spelling bee because you were traumatized by the attention of being a spelling freak, like I did. When you're constantly worried about how others might see you, rather than how you see yourself, the time to gain experiences and to simply *be* is stolen.

There's this thing in quantum physics called the observer effect, which basically states that particles behave differently when they're being observed for study compared to when they're out in the wild. People are just a pile of sensitive, sticky particles. Focusing on *what you are*, instead of just *being*, changes your behavior. And Asian Americans like me who are forced to interrogate themselves so early on can split into both the particle and the titular Observer. In the struggle to manage how others saw me, I became a coward, afraid of the aforementioned dangers that came from being pancit in a tray of baked ziti. My defense was camouflage. This poor bastard thought blending in—near invisibility—would equal safety. Instead of a wallflower, I would become the wall. I begged my parents to buy me Paulie Walnuts–esque velour pants, even though they draped over my skinny waist like velvet curtains. I tried hiding the Filipino side of me behind those curtains. Titas and titos flattened into aunts and uncles. Instead of Filipino food, I asked my mom to make only the Italian dishes she learned from her coworkers. I started covering my face when I laughed, because I didn't like how my narrowed eyes and flared nose made me look more Filipino. I went so far as to lie to my schoolmates and said I was part Sicilian, because I'd heard Sicilians have darker skin like me. (By the way, did you know that in Sicily, to this day, horses are a normal part of the diet? No judgment, it just would have been nice to set Vinny's expectations before he passed on the lechon. His loss.)

I compartmentalized each of my identities and feelings instead of being one human person. Pent-up waves of anger, resentment, jealousy, and sadness would get taken out almost entirely on my poor parents. I couldn't take it out on my peers—that would require me to express my own opinions and feelings in public. Could you imagine?

So, the bruises on my arms remained a secret, only getting flashed to those who made them—my "friends"—like a wristband to get into a club I was going to have a miserable time inside. To the outside world, I was the "quiet Asian nerd," reinforcing the same fucking stereotypes that led to my torment in the first place.

This path can be unintentionally shepherded by parents like my mom, who, in her own immigrant experience, had to swallow pain just to stay afloat in a foreign world. If she had slowed down for even a second out of fear or doubt, she might have hopped on the next twenty-hour flight back to Cebu and I might not exist. She's the most headstrong person I know. A few years ago, I sought her empathy while confronting a hostile, racist work environment. My father had died unexpectedly a month earlier, so I needed her refuge more than ever. She responded by telling me that her friends still made fun of her accent at work. "That's just the way it is," she asserted. In other words, suck it up, the same way I'd dealt with my bruises. An echo of my father's "Say you're American" advice. What's more American than covering up abuse in exchange for a minimized existence?

You might be thinking I'm some sort of science genius because I made that quantum physics reference earlier, but I actually thrived in English classes, particularly in creative writing. A blank page represented something equal parts exhilarating and terrifying: a space free of outside influence and the arbitrary rules I thought I needed to survive. I was afraid to explore that freedom—that would require me to be vulnerable and lean into the Other.

Math, on the other hand, felt safe. Numbers didn't ask for an original point of view. Numbers just sat there, being all orderly and whatnot. Numbers followed all the rules. So, I studied accounting and finance in college, which allowed me to stare at a computer all day with minimal human interaction. To put it nicely: I fucking hated every second of every accounting class I took (that I was awake for). I talked myself into the ludicrous idea that maybe once I started a real-world job, I'd warm up to it. It took two-plus years of routine happy hours to help forget the previous ten to finally hit the panic button. After passing all four parts of the C.P.A. exam, I never sent in the registration paperwork. The idea of "Mark Kramer, C.P.A." made me physically ill. Out of a rock-bottom depression, I started a meandering online blog, which led to an advertising job where I finally had the free time to start taking sketch comedy classes. Now, eight years later, I'm writing dick jokes for an Emmy-winning TV show. And at the risk of jinxing it all . . . it fucking rules. Despite having an English teacher and aspiring novelist for a father, it never crossed my mind that I could live this life. Things like fulfillment and happiness were for other people, not Other people. Indiana Jones got the girl, the glory, and a bunch of sequels. Short Round got lost in that big warehouse with the Ark and the rest of Hollywood's disposable sidekicks.

None of this success was inevitable. There's no definitive "Master's in Accounting–to–Emmy-winner" pipeline in place. The only clear-cut step forward was to stop trying to conform to an impossible ideal and to start being me. What I wish I'd known about the assimilation trap is that no matter how hard I hit the *g*'s in "gabagool" and "gala-mad," I would never actually be seen as one of them. When you play by the rules of white America, your success is still defined by the boundaries of a society ruled almost exclusively by white people for centuries. Not to mention, seeking proximity to whiteness only helps perpetuate a racist hierarchy that has resulted in white people on top since the history of forever. As soon as I started defining my own success—to have fun writing comedy and maybe get paid for it one day—all that excess noise finally reduced to a manageable hum.

Here's the big fucking joke. Are you sitting down? Here we go: If some stranger is asking, "What are you?" they're not actually thinking about *you* at all. Not as a human being, at least—they've already ground you into a two-dimensional Other. It doesn't matter how you respond because they've already answered the question for themselves: *You're not like me.* And while you're still reeling from getting asked, whether for the first time or the thousandth, they're already onto their next useless thought. What might contribute to an existential crisis for an Asian American kid is a forgettable exchange to them. That's quite the fucking burden, and it shouldn't be. Steven Yeun summed it up with a line I'll one day tattoo on my forehead: "Sometimes I wonder if the Asian-American experience is what it's like when you're thinking about everyone else, but nobody else is thinking about you." They have taken our dignity, our sense of belonging, our food, our art, but they should stay the fuck away from our head space. Trust me, instead of writing about this, I'd love to rank the lumpia options near my new home in Los Angeles (Point-Point Joint!). But here I am, in my thirties, still dwelling on childhood trauma. We have to reclaim our head space.

Maybe worst of all, facing The Question pushes you further away from the real answer to "What are you?" In my case, more time and money spent getting sick fades and studying for the C.P.A. exam equaled less writing. Layers upon layers of processed American bullshit get inserted between who you think you should be and who you really are. Only after six-plus years of therapy have I been able to begin to undo all those superfluous layers. That shit is expensive! I want the next generation to avoid the mistakes I made. I still see it happening to my younger cousins, to strangers on Reddit, and in quiet moments in my own head.

Catching up on my culture as an adult—through learning to cook chicken adobo, reading books by Asian American writers who are way better at doing words than I am, taking Filipino-language classes with friends, embracing the AAPI writer community, and mentoring the up-and-comers who will one day take my job—has been rewarding. Sometimes, I daresay, for the first time in my life, I feel like a whole person. But I can't help but feel like I wasted two decades of my life chasing someone else's dream. The "American dream." Why did I ever let anyone else determine what my dreams looked like? I'm American too. And defining that identity by my own terms has been so much more gratifying than the quest for acceptance. Of course, saying I'm American doesn't mean I'm about to wave the flag around and cover up my shameful history. I choose to embrace the confused kid I grew out of and learn from his mistakes. And the next time I get asked the question "What are you?" by a stranger, I want to finally show that kid the correct answer: "None of your fucking business."

Working While Asian

by Ellen K. Pao

When I think about growing up Asian in America, I remember family gatherings with homemade dumpling-eating contests, birthday celebrations with way too many photos, and my grandmother's dramatic tales of hard work and kindness being rewarded after a long struggle. My parents tried to bring these tales to life in how they raised us. When my friends went away to summer camps, my sisters and I stayed home, doing math problem sets and writing weekly book reports. Instead of Sunday school or Hebrew school, we had Chinese school, which meant more homework and studying.

My favorite childhood experiences were also othering, and teachers, following common practice back then, advocated strongly for us to assimilate. We were the first Asian family in our New Jersey elementary school, and my sister's kindergarten teacher instructed my parents to stop speaking in Chinese to us at home. My parents did so—it was normal to follow the teachers' lead, to obey authority, to assume they knew what they were doing. Saturday Chinese school, with an hour of language studies and an hour of cultural studies, gave us only two hours a week to counterbalance the dozens of hours we spent in school trying to shrink our Asian identities.

I was raised, along with a whole generation of immigrants' children, to believe in meritocracy, that working hard was all that mattered at school and at work. My parents came out of the Taiwanese educational system, where college admissions depended only on how you scored on the entrance exam. They studied intensely for that test, which determined what college they went to, what major they studied, and what careers they could pursue. They did well and after college won scholarships and stipends from US graduate schools. The meritocracy worked for them. And so they passed it down: if you do your job, don't complain, and keep your head down, you will be rewarded. I learned to be modest and not self-promotional; I learned to give credit and not to take it. And I learned to *chi ku*, to swallow any bitterness, so when I wasn't rewarded fairly, I didn't complain—I just worked harder.

I was in my thirties by the time I realized with complete clarity how much meritocracy was a myth in the United States. I had struggled with addressing inconsistent feedback at my job at a venture capital firm. I didn't know how to both "be louder and own the room!" while also making myself smaller because "you're too assertive . . . and your elbows are too pointy!" I remember the day it finally made sense— that working hard and being good at my job was not enough. The firm announced a critical round of promotions for its next fund—a huge one—and in this announcement none of us women were promoted and almost all the men were. The women were much stronger candidates on paper—more experienced, more educated, more years of tenure. And after one woman analyzed the financial performance of our investments, it was clear we were better at our jobs too.

The promotion of even one woman would have made the unfairness harder to identify. But when none were promoted—and the leaders of the firm were all male—I realized that there was no meritocracy in those promotion decisions. No level of experience, education, or success would have gotten us those promotions. It was a wake-up call for me to stop internalizing structural problems as my own failures and to start working on solving them systemically. I felt a wide range of emotions, starting with anger and frustration at the huge obstacles we faced, mixed in with relief at finally figuring out that the problem wasn't me—it was the leaders of the firm and the venture capital industry. That insight freed me from trying to live up to the meritocracy myth. I could now focus on my work instead of spending time and energy trying to anticipate the negative feedback, inconsistent responses, and additional new requirements that seemed to follow every accomplishment I achieved and stymie all my attempts to succeed.

I looked back at my earlier experiences and realized why my suggestions never worked. When I called attention internally to the problems of sexism, I was told to gather the women together to talk about them among ourselves. When I tried to negotiate my salary, I was called a complainer who should be more grateful. When I eventually sued the firm for discrimination and retaliation, they fired me. When the news leaked, the press mostly took their side and I was publicly branded a poor performer and a liar. Friends and colleagues went cold; they weren't up for being blackballed with me, and I understand why. For half a year, the only person who even talked about maybe hiring me wanted me to help invest in Brazilian climate change start-ups, when I didn't understand Brazilian culture or speak Portuguese, and when my focus was enterprise and consumer tech. I learned how deep and broad the systemic problems were across the tech industry by living them. I got a job from Reddit, only because the CEO thought orthogonally and wasn't afraid of risk or working outside the system.

More recently, I discovered how the model minority myth has been used to perpetuate these systems by serving as an effective wedge to distance Asians from other communities. I wish I had understood earlier how the myth pits Asians against other racial groups, especially the Black community. When Asians talk about more policing against anti-Asian hate, it's a tangible effect of the hate that sprouts from fractionalization. When we harm other communities, we harm ourselves.

Often it was hard to tell whether people were othering and excluding me based on my gender or race, but I saw clearly that being an Asian woman was a problem. I remember being excluded from board meetings at Reddit, even when I was CEO, and from team meetings at a venture capitalist firm, groups of just a handful of people. When I was in talks to become CEO of Reddit, one of my colleagues refused to report to me. He said he wanted me to be CEO and that he wanted to help me succeed, but when push came to shove, he would not recognize me as his leader. Maybe I should have cared more, but I was focused on getting the job done as I was raised to do. And I did. The team nearly doubled in size, and users grew 50 percent. We cleaned house internally: We found and built out new office space, we created and shared company values, we took a stand against sexual harassment with training, and we held a few days of company all-hands meetings to reinforce our new values and culture. We started performance reviews and created better processes for departing employees. We created and implemented salary ranges and job levels for fair compensation. We got rid of unauthorized nude photos and revenge porn, and most of the rest of the internet followed us. We were first to ban harassment—successfully—and to acknowledge and include cross-platform activities as part of that. We started and published our first privacy report on requests for user information and content removal. We even raised $250,000 for Nepal's earthquake relief efforts.

I share all these accomplishments because I feel a need to shed the modesty and humility that were core to my upbringing but that worked against me. With time, I've realized that it's important to let people know what you've done, because too many others will take credit for it otherwise. And if others don't know what you've accomplished, they often won't figure it out. Instead, the opportunities will go to the person who *is* willing to take credit, and it's not only you but also your team that gets overlooked in the process. At Reddit, it was a huge team effort to accomplish all that we did in an incredibly short amount of time, all of it with tremendous personal risk—they should get credit for the work. I believe we were so effective because we had built a diverse and inclusive management team in nine short months: two Latinx women, a Black woman, a Muslim man, a white-Latinx woman, an Asian man, two white men, plus me, an Asian woman. Most have left, but they still deserve credit.

I also share these accomplishments because I got fired despite all the work I did, and it is more evidence that the meritocracy is a myth. I thought getting to the top position at a growing start-up and really transforming it on so many levels would be rewarded, not punished. I thought I didn't have to talk about my results, because they would stand on their own. After I was forced to resign, I felt alone in my experience, thinking that the backstabbing, and ultimately firing, was because of their discomfort with a woman leader. But then I started reading about Asian American CEOs stepping down unexpectedly, and eventually learned from them directly that they were asked or told to leave. The reasons for their forced departures weren't consistent with their results or the feedback they had received earlier, just like in my own experience. And our treatment is completely inconsistent with the many chances that white male CEOs and founders with much less to show and much worse behavior have been given time and time again. It has been so demotivating to see Asian CEO after Asian CEO reach the top level and continue to succeed only to be shot down and pushed out.

Even after realizing the tech industry is built on barriers to progress for Asians—along with Black people, Latinx people, Indigenous people, women, nonbinary people, transgender people, disabled people, and so many others—I continue to have hope for the future and work to accelerate change in the tech industry. To that end, I cofounded Project Include with Erica Joy Baker, bethanye McKinney Blount, Tracy Chou, Laura Gómez, Y-Vonne Hutchinson, Freada Kapor Klein, and Susan Wu, who have become trusted advisers. We designed Project Include to give tech leaders an understanding of the structures and biases that block marginalized communities and to provide actionable and meaningful solutions. Our mission is to give everyone in tech a fair chance to succeed. I work alongside amazing nonprofit leaders who are pushing for systemic change beyond the leadership level, including Catherine Bracy of TechEquity Collaborative, Kimberly Bryant of Black Girls CODE, Janet Haven of Data & Society, Karla Monterrosa formerly of Code2040, and Aniyia Williams formerly of Black & Brown Founders.

And I draw inspiration from within the Asian community when our leaders speak up for other communities. Asians for Black Lives conversations have been led by people such as activist Michelle Kim and tech leader Skye Lee. They deftly navigate the complexity of being Asian in America—the privileges and the barriers—and use their privilege to knock down barriers for everyone. It's not a coincidence that the first wave of people who sued tech companies such as Twitter, Facebook, and Betterworks for discrimination were Asian women: Tina Huang, Chia Hong, and Beatrice Kim.

I'm inspired by the many people speaking up at great personal cost, at professional cost, usually losing a well-paying, stable job, because they see inequities and because they want to change the industry, people such as Timnit Gebru, Ifeoma Ozoma, Aerica Shimizu Banks, Ingrid Avendaño, Ana Medina, Liz Fong, and Kelly Ellis. I know they are changing the industry with their leadership, and that companies and tech leaders are paying attention. CEOs will have to learn from our stories and fix these problems, or they're going to have to get out of the way to make room for leaders who understand that in the near future everyone really will get a fair chance to succeed based on their contributions and capabilities instead of navigating barriers of discrimination and biases. Only then will our hard work, successful results, and advocacy be rewarded instead of punished.

Facing Myself

by David Kwong

I saw my first magician in a pumpkin patch in Rochester, New York. I was there with my dad, who is Chinese and who grew up in Hong Kong. He had settled into a faculty position at the University of Rochester Medical Center after immigrating to Canada for college and a Ph.D. in biochemistry. Rochester, which became my hometown, was also where my mother, a Jewish professor of American history, had grown up. Every fall, Dad and I would visit Bauman's Farm to get cider and donuts, play on haystacks, and pick apples. When I was ten, there was the added attraction of a magician performing in the barn, an addition that would change the course of my life.

The bald and bespectacled conjurer demonstrated one of the greatest tricks in the annals of magic: the sponge ball trick. He placed a little red sponge ball in my hand, made a second one disappear, and when I opened my hand I miraculously had both of them. *Mind blown.* The magician then performed the trick on my father. When my father opened his fist to reveal the two sponge balls, I turned to the omniscient biochemist and asked, "How did that work?" He flashed me a sheepish grin, shrugged his shoulders, and said, "I have no idea."

And that's when I knew that I wanted to be a magician.

First, I had to finish elementary and middle school. I lived in a relatively affluent suburb with an excellent educational system that affirmed the values of ethnic and racial diversity. My Chinese and Jewish heritages mixed easily. We were involved in the local Reform Jewish temple, and when it came time for my Bar Mitzvah all my friends enjoyed the reception at a Chinese restaurant. (You may not be surprised that my Jewish and Chinese relatives were equally thrilled about the Chinese food.) During Chanukah, my family devoured potato latkes topped with my father's delicious soy sauce and white pepper concoction. Still, despite the culture of acceptance surrounding me, I couldn't help but want to fit in with the soccer and lacrosse players—all of whom were white—who sat together smugly in the "cool section" of the middle school cafeteria. I, too, wanted to be popular, but how could that happen for a sensitive, scrawny, violin-playing half-Chinese, half-Jewish kid? Perhaps all teenagers have some of this insecurity, but no matter how progressive or enlightened their environment, the children of immigrants or minorities often feel this desire for acceptance more intensely. Certainly, this was true for me.

When I got to high school, I figured out that playing Scrabble and doing card tricks on the non-cool side of the lunchroom, with other kids like me, made me happier. These were the nerds, with whom I fit right in with my brains and interests. During any given study hall, you could find me with my nose in a magic book or memorizing lists of Scrabble two-letter words.

In college, that continued. I cofounded the Harvard Magic Club (with fellow undergraduate and now psychologist Adam Grant) and performed shows around the campus. I wanted to immerse myself in the world of illusion, but alas, magic wasn't a major at Harvard. This is when I first noticed a tension between my passion for magic and a more conventional career path. It seemed as if my parents and everyone around me were encouraging me to become a doctor, lawyer, or academic—professions that historically have enabled upward mobility for both Chinese and Jewish families. In truth, I too was skeptical of an artistic career, especially one that might dead-end in working the birthday-party circuit. And so, I settled on concentrating in American history, planning to focus my studies on the rarely told stories of conjurers from the Golden Age of magic (the 1880s to the 1930s). It seemed like a good plan; I could dive into a subject matter of great interest to me while keeping the door open for law school or graduate studies.

Eventually, I wrote an honors thesis about Asian impersonation in magic shows: white magicians who employed "Oriental" themes and even pretended to be Asian themselves. This "yellow face" enhanced the exoticism of their acts while at the same time mocking Eastern cultures. For example, Chung Ling Soo was one of the most celebrated magicians of the early 1900s. After his untimely death by misadventure (a bullet catch trick gone wrong), it was revealed to the public that he was a white American man of Scottish descent named William Robinson. My college research started me thinking about some big questions. Must Asians always be consigned to the role of the exotic other? Do Asians have to behave onstage the way white people imagine and want them to be? Can an Asian performer portray a strong figure instead of being relegated to the part of the humorous sidekick? Up to this point, I had not struggled with matters of my own ethnic identity, because my environments had been so accepting, but my research raised an additional question. If I, as a person who is both Asian and white, was performing onstage, whom should I be portraying? Whom would I be expected to portray? If I went ahead with my magician dream, would I have to grapple with these issues? Would I, unlike many Asian actors, have choices about whom I could be onstage? I wondered about this particularly because there were no Asian American magicians in the public eye when I graduated in 2002.

After college, still undecided between a conventional and unconventional career, I headed to New York City to make my way into the business side of entertainment, which seemed more exciting than law and more stable than being a magician. I landed a job at HBO, but after two great years the persistent matter of who I was convinced me to learn more about my Asian heritage. Even though I had always participated in Kwong family activities like visits to giant dim sum restaurants and red envelope exchanges, I wanted to delve more deeply into what it meant to be Chinese. So, I quit my position and moved to Hong Kong, where I still had Kwong family relatives. And this sojourn seemed like the perfect opportunity to dabble in the unconventional and perhaps turn my childhood hobby into my adult livelihood. My parents responded with disbelief: "What?! You're quitting your job to become a magician?!" But I had some passions to follow.

Once there, I practiced sleight of hand over late-night bowls of noodles. I demonstrated my magic prowess at bars and private clubs. I staged one-man shows for Hong Kong's banks and private equity firms to pay for more late-night bowls of noodles. Most important, I traveled to the Sichuan province to learn from an elderly master magician a renowned trick called *bian lian* (face changing). This trick is considered a national secret and involves a cowled opera performer changing his colorful terra-cotta masks at lightning speed.

One second he might be displaying a red face, and with a flick of a fan the mask becomes green. Then he turns it yellow, orange, purple, magenta—each face with a different design as he cycles through dozens of countenances, shape-shifting from character to character. This art form combines timing and choreography and takes a lifetime to perfect. Full of youthful hubris, I thought I could master it in ten days. I was wrong. (To this day, the masks sit in my closet unused.) But the trick acquired a larger meaning in the process, a metaphorical one, helping me to answer the questions that had been weighing on me. I realized I did not have to put on a social mask, adapting my identity to other people's expectations depending on the circumstances. Simultaneously, it affirmed for me that I was a person with multiple identities. And that I could be true to them all. As an Asian American performer, I did not need to comply with other people's needs to reduce me to one thing. Even though there were no Asian American magicians on the scene, I knew what I loved and could pursue it on my own terms.

With a new sense of confidence and direction, I returned to the United States and eventually established myself as a magician in Los Angeles. I fashioned a magic show out of the things I loved the most: Scrabble, puzzles, and history. I was David Kwong. Proud to represent Asians onstage and at the same time to be my multifaceted self. Our current commitment to diversity across the entertainment industry and in America as a whole means that performers are free to show their actual faces. Asian magicians can draw on the rich traditions of their cultures without needing to play into stereotypes. Of course, we aren't completely there yet as a society, and I have more to discover about myself. Perhaps understanding one's identity is a lifelong project.

Shortly before it opened, I asked Constance Wu to help me promote my one-man show, *The Enigmatist*, to Asian Americans by stressing that I was an Asian American performer. She wisely replied, "David, just be you and your identity will shine through. That's the best thing that you can do to represent us." That is my advice, as well. Show your unmasked face, and the uniqueness of who you are will be all the magic you need.

When I'm here in America, I can feel this constant protest, like, *I'm not just a Korean person, I'm an American person.*

—STEVEN YEUN

Places

by Gayle Gaviola

My Filipino father served thirty years in the United States Air Force. We changed towns every few years, turning our relocations into family road trips and crisscrossing America while I bickered with my brother in the backseat to a soundtrack of "Smooth Operator" and "Lovely Day." We built countless fond memories together across state lines, at budget hotels, and in small towns with revolving names amid a steady backdrop of white faces. We met a lot of military families in endless transit like ourselves, and my brother and I became quite fearless at forming fast friendships, saying good-bye, and welcoming our next adventure. Much of my identity needed to be built over various area codes, and a side effect of this upbringing was that I learned the importance of knowing myself when my surroundings remained fluid. Family was my constant companion and chief source of emotional fuel; our love was rooted in simply spending time together, no matter where in the world we were. And so, home became a state of mind rather than a place. As I think back to the many places I've lived, particularly as a Filipino American, certain memories stand out.

Virginia. I was in first grade when I decided I wanted to be Cinderella for Halloween. The costume we bought at the supermarket came with a full-face plastic mask of white skin, animated yellow hair, and eyeholes. I wore it proudly over my brown face while trick-or-treating, thinking that a girl without white skin or blond hair simply couldn't be a real Cinderella. (Her eyes *could* be brown, though.)

Washington State. I was in fifth grade when I realized there were parts of my upbringing that were Other. It was Multicultural Potluck Day, and our teacher encouraged everyone to bring in homemade dishes from their respective family cultures. I was pumped to bring my mom's Philippine cassava cake, which I loved . . . until a friend took a bite of it and commented, "Something about that doesn't go together. It's weird." He innocently dropped it in the trash to try some other dishes. My mom's cake remained one of the least eaten by day's end, and it singed my insides with humiliation.

"It's weird" burned into my mind, and over time I convinced myself that maybe cassava cake wasn't even all that. If something I loved didn't "go together" in the context of an American classroom, why did *I* love it so much?

Southern California. I was in seventh grade when I met a box of four-dollar ColorSilk, thus beginning a years-long affair of dyeing my hair blond. Maybe it was the memory of how natural slipping on that Cinderella mask felt, but I thought blond hair simply elevated my look. When my hair was light, my features brightened, my skin looked luminous, and the rest of me just seemed lighter, more vibrant. Better? It was a compulsion born in the early 2000s that would last for decades and never truly leave me.

Southern Illinois. I was in eighth grade, living in a mostly white cornfield town, when I saw a brown girl on the blacktop. I asked her if she was Filipino too—she was. Pre-Illinois, I hadn't ever had a Filipina friend, so I was exhilarated to finally see myself in a peer. I felt a sisterhood with this girl before ever knowing her name. She would become my best friend and stay so beyond high school; I would eventually be her maid of honor. Back then, I'd never had a friendship where so much about my family upbringing need not be explained, where having a friend over for dinner wasn't some big educational event if my mom made Filipino food. We also happened to share several physical and personality characteristics, which I found myself appreciating as we blended into Midwest Americana. We both joined the dance team. Outside of school, we worked the same jobs at Hollister and Applebee's. When coworkers and classmates frequently mixed us up, despite her having braces and short hair at one point and me . . . not having those things, we would just giggle. We started telling everyone we were twins. Mostly because it was funny, but also deep down maybe we believed it was easier to laugh it off than to correct people who couldn't tell the difference between us. And I was used to feeling different, so belonging to a team felt fantastic. Why rock the boat if we were both loved?

As middle and high school progressed, I found myself building more Asian friendships. Not that our town had many Asian American people. But perhaps all five Asians in our grade saw one another and liked how it felt to be seen.

• • •

Central California. I was a college freshman when I learned that Asian American interest sororities were a thing. My small midwestern town's definition of "Cool Girl" had turned me into a tan blonde who loved punk rock and *The OC*, and who imagined herself as the "beauty queen of only eighteen" whom Adam Levine was singing to on *Songs About Jane.* Now I was surrounded by a community of women who looked like me, had interests all over the map, and were completely comfortable in their brown skin. A stark contrast to my Illinois mindset of blending in with white community and culture. What the hell? I craved their unapologetic self-awareness. I became friends with brilliant, beautiful Filipino, Vietnamese, Korean, Chinese, and Japanese American women. I found relief in a community where I could focus on celebrating my culture and shared experiences with so many others, instead of blending into another majority. I didn't have to pretend I was someone's twin to feel a sense of belonging. For the first time, I could just be.

My high-school friends started asking me if all my friends were Asian, which they were. And I fell for and dated an Asian boy. A small part of me worried: am I losing touch with the white-friendly image I'd worked so hard to build back in Illinois? Will diving headfirst into my Asianness rinse away all that effort? I found myself worrying whether I was becoming "too Asian" and letting go of my "true" self, while simultaneously feeling mad and guilty that my mind would even go there.

My curiosity grew. I let it. I joined and eventually became president of that Asian American interest sorority. I took so many Asian American Studies classes for fun that I accidentally became an Asian American Studies minor. I would eventually go on to work for a major media company, where I would cochair its Asian American & Pacific Islander employee resource group.

Since then, I wish I could say these experiences have gifted me magical license to stop caring so much about how I'm perceived. Or that after a tumultuous year for all Asians and people of color compounded by a global pandemic, I am now an Unbothered Woke AAPI Woman who fully understands her identity while diligently fighting the good fight for all marginalized groups. The truth is, I'm still bothered, I still have so much to learn, and I struggle to place my emotions every day.

Los Angeles. I was twenty-two years old when I became an entertainment publicist despite seeing no leaders in the industry who looked like me. Something that made me feel both special and anxious.

New York. I was twenty-five years old when I moved to the city and was asked by a senior executive where I was "from from." Something that made me feel both pissed and defiant.

Miami. I was thirty-three years old when I crossed the street with my white boyfriend-now-fiancé and a group of Asian dudes walked by. One of them yelled, "Date an Asian guy!" and threw us a judgy look. As if I were abandoning my people by being with someone I love. Something that made me feel both deflated and annoyed.

I've spent most of my life convincing myself and others that I belong in the spaces I enter. The ironic flip side to this is I've simultaneously criticized myself for how or why I should express these things. Am I caring too much, caring too little, expressing myself the "right" way?

Over time, I've realized that the simultaneous pride, confusion, and guilt I carry is specific to the Asian American and Pacific Islander experience. Maybe all three feelings are just meant to coexist.

Here is what I know.

To be Asian American is a tremendous honor, an ongoing journey I both fully embrace and will never fully understand.

I am Filipina American. My story is one of millions, and that is the only one I will ever truly know.

And in the tapestry of Asian America, Filipino Americans are one shade of the Asian and Pacific Islander experience. At the same time, what an honor it is to be connected to something so much larger than ourselves—a fabric of resilient, family-first dreamers who use their actions, sacrifices, and food to show love, often in favor of words.

Words are largely how I make my living now. And if I had the words back then, I would tell that first grader in Virginia she didn't need that mask to be Cinderella. (Shout-out Brandy and Camila Cabello.)

I would tell that fifth grader in Washington that she doesn't need a reason to love something she enjoys. And more leftovers just means more for her.

I would tell that seventh grader in California to brace herself for the photos she'll look back on years later. Something called Facebook, then Instagram, will chronicle her hair choices in perpetuity.

I would tell that eighth grader in Illinois to hug her best friend tight, and that the best is yet to come. And that there is power in correcting those who are too lazy to see you as an individual.

I would thank that college student in California for finding the courage to fall deeper into herself.

I am not the places I've lived or the food I eat. I am not my skin, my hair, my friends, my partner, my job. Not individually, anyway. I am a proud military brat, a daughter, a sister, an aunt, a soon-to-be-wife, a friend, a forever student. I am everything I've said and intentionally left unsaid. I am everything that has ever made me laugh, and everything that has ever made me cry. And regardless of where life takes me, I belong here.

So do you.

My First Rodeo

by Yoonj Kim

My parents did this thing when I was a kid that drove me nuts: they'd compare everything under the sun to Korean culture.

Their attachments to the homeland were boundless, liable to appear out of nowhere—delighting over deli pickles that tasted like oijim, clamoring over gemstone rings at the mall that looked like *garakji*, only allowing a puppy if it was a jindo, the national dog of Korea. It didn't matter where we were. They never failed to hype my birth country every chance they got.

I did not like this. I did not like it at all.

I was born in Seoul but had moved to the United States when I was five. I wanted so badly to be an American kid, not an immigrant stuck in the past. As far as I was concerned, Umma and Appa were getting in the way of my assimilation into the fabulous American dream I longed to be welcomed into. I felt like I was so close, too, because I rarely faced blatant discrimination. In fact, I was reminded that I was an outsider more often by their constant Koreanization than by strangers, making me silently resent them whenever they brought it up in public.

Umma and Appa moved us from Seoul to Boston so that Appa could earn a specialization in prosthodontics after working as a general dentist. Umma had enjoyed a glamorous career as an anchorwoman but gave it up for America, where the audience would think she sounded like an outsider. She gracefully accepted her new fate without complaint and soon gave birth to my little sister, Yoona, the first American citizen in our family. We eventually would have returned to South Korea were it not for the 1997 Asian financial crisis, after which my parents decided it would be more prudent to try our luck here than back home. At the time, California was one of only a couple states that allowed immigrants with foreign undergraduate degrees to practice dentistry. So off to the land of palm trees we went.

In Boston, my precious Saturday mornings had been spent watching *Arthur* and feeding breadcrumbs to pigeons from our little fifth-story balcony. But once we arrived in the boiling melting pot of Los Angeles, my parents enrolled Yoona and me in Korean school, doomed to attend every Saturday morning for the next ten years. You'd think they would have taken this step in lily-white New England, but no, it wasn't until we moved smack into the middle of the largest Korean population in the United States that my parents suddenly acted like we had to learn more about our culture. I was seven when I started and loathed having to spend weekends slogging through Korean passages while other kids played. Yet no matter how much I complained, Umma and Appa were steadfast.

"You'll understand later," Umma said, to which I rolled my eyes.

"You're Korean, Yoonju. Don't forget," Appa added, and by then my eyes had rolled to the back of my head.

Why couldn't they understand that we lived in America now?

Korean school marked the beginning of my awareness that I was different from my "regular school" classmates, who didn't have to spend their weekends languishing in another classroom. My burgeoning immigrant's insecurity paired with a desire to fit in spurred my attempts to be American the only way I knew how—superficially. Like adding "dude" to my vocabulary. Wearing cut-off Roxy short shorts. Dropping my Korean name and going by "Jean," as in Jean Grey from X-Men, my favorite superhero.

By the time I began middle school, we had moved an hour south of LA to Orange County, settling in a conservative suburb of mostly whites and Hispanics. I took my cues from the girls at school I considered cool—and cool to me was understanding the culture. Cool was knowing what was up. I didn't feel I possessed either quality. I was the kid who joined Girl Scout Brownies after Umma told me it must be a baking club, quietly dropping out after the first meeting. My goal was to at least *look* like I knew what I was doing.

So, I became a chameleon. I adjusted my appearance and behavior to blend in with my surroundings. And it kind of worked. My ability to adapt provided a comforting Band-Aid over an aching vulnerability, a raw fear I couldn't shake that no matter how well I might pass as American on the outside, there was some inherent inner quality I would never possess.

Social camouflage is both a superpower and a curse for many Asian Americans, especially those of East Asian heritage. On a physical level, it's a loaded form of privilege that allows us access into white-dominated culture simply because the color of our skin means we stand out less. It's also a situational crutch due to the conflicting multitudes of Asian stereotypes—essentially considered to be so good at everything (except driving) that we're celebrated for nothing. If you think about it, Asian Americans are the only minority that encompass both white- and blue-collar tropes, from us all being a doctor or engineer and also a massage parlor worker. It bestows this unique ability to pass through a range of socioeconomic environments due to the encompassing lower- *and* upper-class stereotypes that onlookers project onto us.

"Honorary Whites" was an actual designation in apartheid South Africa, reserved for the supposedly wealthy Asians whose home countries, like Korea and Japan, benefited South African trade. The Chinese were classified as Coloured, a secondary sociopolitical status between Whites and Blacks. I found this out during a college journalism residency in Johannesburg when an Afrikaans taxi driver casually asked, "Are you Chinese? Or Japanese?"

"I'm Korean, actually. Korean American."

"Ah! During apartheid, Koreans were Honorary Whites, too, like the Japanese. The Chinese were not. Funny, *nè*?"

Maybe it was my suspicious imagination, but he seemed to regard me more easily after our exchange. I'd be lying if I didn't confess I felt slightly relieved, too, a self-interested complacency instead of outrage at the codified racism, because that's what social engineering does. It makes us feel safe for not *feeling* like outsiders even though we inherently, irredeemably are.

This is what makes social camouflage a curse. It's an illusion, one that is destined to crack.

As a confused teenager in Southern California, though, I was living the illusion. The cracks began to appear because of my obsession with horses. Among a typical Asian schedule of violin, piano, and after-school math lessons, horseback riding was the one activity I did that was undeniably American. Looking back now, I can see that it was also my chameleonic attempt to be seen as an honorary white, long before I knew such a term existed.

I'd taken riding lessons in LA from a Korean instructor. That my parents insisted on a Korean influence even in this extracurricular activity was highly irritating, as by then I'd gotten a handle on presenting myself as a California girl in Hurley tanks and Rainbow flip-flops. He didn't turn out to be a great teacher, though, so when we moved to Orange County they agreed to let me try a new instructor I'd found, a white woman who specialized in Andalusians, a gorgeous Spanish breed that look like unicorns. She'd sounded friendly when I talked to her on the phone (I'd told her my name was Jean). The first time we met in person, she greeted us with a tight smile. I didn't read too much into her forced pleasantry, nor did Umma. Perhaps Umma recognized this woman's bias but chose not to say anything because I was so deliriously excited. Our meeting ended with the instructor inviting us to a competition that weekend in LA.

On Sunday morning, I ran into Umma and Appa's room to wake them up so they could drive us the hour into town. The arena was packed when we arrived. The instructor was with a group of people in cowboy boots hanging around a young girl atop a show horse. With Umma and Appa behind me, I bounced up to her in my breeches and boots.

The group turned to stare. The instructor's face changed from a genuine smile to the same tight one she'd given us at our initial meeting. That's how I could tell it was fake this time. She wasn't a shy smiler. She just wasn't happy to see us.

Her posse gave us confused looks. Not a single one of them made a move to say hello. My palms felt cold. I suddenly felt acutely self-conscious that Umma, Appa, and I were the only Asians—actually, the only nonwhites—in this dusty arena of subtle hostility blanketed under the innocence of horses.

"Oh, hey, Jean. Nice that you came," she said with a flaccid look as she led the horse and group away, not bothering to introduce us to anyone. She didn't look back, and we didn't follow.

A searing humiliation consumed me. Umma and Appa looked disturbed and were at a loss as to what to say. I didn't blame them. I knew that if we were back in Korea, or even in Koreatown speaking in their native language, my parents would have pressed the instructor about her behavior. But here their hands and tongues were tied. My heart sank with shame for having dragged them into this undignified situation just so I could play cowgirl. I struggled but failed to find the words to expel these unfamiliar emotions as we walked back to the car in silence.

Horseback riding was supposed to be my way of proving I was American too. I wanted so badly to be an equestrian, the classic symbol of Wild West Americana. And while my love of horses was genuine, this reasoning was yet another superficial attempt to blend in. Only this time, I wasn't able to pull off the chameleonic transformation.

The rejection tore through my self-esteem, making me believe that I wasn't enough on some intrinsic level. Still, I naively showed up for a few lessons, as if I could prove with my riding skills that they were wrong about me, only to have the instructor ride around on her own horse most of the time, leaving me by myself. Riding is a spiritual exercise that involves bonding with the animal, but because of my external preoccupation I forgot to look inward. Taking those lessons robbed me of my love of horses for a while.

A couple months passed. One day, at the end of another useless lesson, the instructor told Umma and me that it wasn't working out and that we should consider finding a new teacher. I immediately felt as if it were me who was lacking—again—that I was such a hopelessly bad rider she had no choice but to let me go. But after I spent a few days reflecting on our lessons—the paid lessons that she rarely supervised—it finally dawned on me that I wasn't the one who was lacking. It was her lazy ass. How could someone who didn't even give me a chance know the extent of my potential?

Nationalists love to tell immigrants to assimilate, that if we acted more "like them," we'd be accepted. But it's like one of those half-hearted invitations where they don't expect you to show up—like at a horse show—and if you do, you're not exactly arriving to open arms and champagne.

America was a fucking tease, and I decided I wasn't that desperate.

From that point on, my sense of self shifted as I woke up from the illusion. I never asked anyone to call me Jean again, and I grew to love my Korean name for its uniqueness. I joined Korean community groups in my free time. And I even started to enjoy it when Umma or Appa made their Korean comparisons in public. I didn't think it was embarrassing anymore. It was delightfully subversive, their way of reminding my sister and me that we came from somewhere. That America was not the first or only place. Even though we *wanted* to be here, we did not *need* it. We were our own people and we were whole, whether or not this new country we'd decided to embrace embraced us back.

Whenever I look back at how I got to this revelation, my mind wanders to those hay-filled stables and a long-forgotten panic, for that was the first time I willfully stepped out of my parents' Korean bubble. It was only once I tumbled back in that I began to understand its empowering authenticity, shielding me from disappearing into a harsh, fickle landscape uninterested in celebrating me as an individual.

Thank you, Umma and Appa, for making sure I never forgot who I was, even when I wanted to.

The Next Draft

by Aneesh Raman

The First Draft

At the beginning, I wasn't American. Even though I was born here, I was Indian. And that made complete sense, not only to others but also to me. The fact that my parents were immigrants meant that I was immigrant-lite, here as a recent recruit, not a real resident.

"What are you?" I'd often get asked when I met someone new. "Indian," I'd reply. "Red dot Indian or war chant Indian?" came the frequent follow-up. "Red dot," I'd answer swiftly and straight-forwardly, eager to avoid a conversation about bindis.

By the time I got to high school, America—and I—had progressed. I started to see myself as a hyphenated American. First, as an *Indian-American*. Then, in college, as a *South Asian–American*. Then, after college, as an *Asian-American*. And that's where I stayed. Happily.

I didn't worry much about not being a real American because I wasn't a real American. That was just a fact. America, for my family and me, was an opportunity, not a home. It was the chance—privilege, even—to make more of our lives than if my parents had stayed in India because in America, anyone from anywhere could do anything.

In my mind, no other country offered that kind of deal, so I embraced it fully and evangelized it constantly. Even as a kid, I believed in American exceptionalism and the idea that this was a singular place with a singular promise that ran through everything from the Declaration of Independence to the Constitution to the final words of the Pledge of Allegiance—"liberty and justice for all." Not for some—for all.

I was not blind to injustice in America. I just believed, as many did, that where injustice persisted, the oppressed always had a means to compel progress, and that, over time, they always did. To me, America's story was one of ever-expanding equality. We didn't always move in a straight line, but we always moved, irreversibly, forward.

I was, however, blind to something else about America. For decades, hiding in plain sight—undeniable yet unspoken to or by me—was the great caveat to the promise of America. To access liberty, justice, opportunity, all of it—fully—you needed to be white.

America has always been a majority white nation. The idea of what it means to be American has always been grounded in the idea of what it means to be white, a connection cemented over centuries by our methodical use of race to categorize and organize us all against a white baseline. So omnipresent is race in America that it's best to see it as a force like gravity, weighing down virtually every aspect of our lives in ways we often don't think about or focus on because it's just the way things are.

That was certainly the case in Wellesley, Massachusetts, the almost entirely white town where I grew up relentlessly assimilating not into America but into white culture in America. I did everything from adopting the local uniform—a polo shirt and khaki pants—to unwittingly inheriting the same detachment that many white Americans exhibit toward the struggles of communities of color. Looking back, I realize a defining experience from high school was turning on my only Indian American friend so that I could be seen as less Other to my white friends. It was an act of both self-rejection and self-advancement.

The rewards of my assimilation were plentiful. By the time I graduated from high school, I had been a leader in more clubs than I can recall, elected Student Congress president, voted "Most Likely to Succeed," and, on graduation day, was awarded the Senior Cup, an award given to a male and female student who represented the best of the class. The Senior Cup was not an award handed out to students on the margins; it was a mainstream award. It was a real American award. I still remember beaming uncontrollably while driving back from graduation that night because winning the Senior Cup meant I had unlocked a new level of acceptance.

Becoming white was working.

I was not alone. Across the country, other Indian Americans were doing the same thing. Knowingly and unknowingly, we were succeeding in America by becoming white in America. Our parents, in ways they also didn't fully realize, had situated us perfectly for that pursuit. Many of them were among a privileged and educated professional class of immigrants, who had benefited greatly from the cruel caste system in India. As a result, they went to the best schools and became the engineers and doctors the United States desperately needed in the late 1960s.

An immigrant wave fueled by those destined for success meant that Indian Americans would soon emerge as a nonthreatening, highly respected minority group. As would other Asian American communities. To simultaneously embrace us and Other us, we became known as the "model minority." Culturally, that term would be used as proof that there was no systemic racism in America, even though that was untrue. Untrue because many of those "model minorities" were only allowed in because of their pedigree. Untrue because many Asian Americans were struggling too. Untrue because, as a community, we enjoyed opportunities that were consistently denied to others, Black, Latinx, and Native Americans in particular.

It's important to note that I was neither indifferent nor antagonistic toward my ethnicity. I just compartmentalized it. I was involved in our Hindu temple, a temple my parents helped found. At Harvard, I was involved in the South Asian Association. After college, I did a Fulbright to India explicitly in search of my roots. I was both proud of my culture and understanding of the limits it imposed on me in terms of becoming a real American.

I did sometimes think about future generations of my family. My descendants, I imagined, would be real Americans. And that mattered deeply to me, because I wanted this country, for them, to be more than an opportunity. I wanted it to be a home. And as a home, the idea that those generations of my family could help shape this country's future was inspiring.

That was the first draft of my story of self and country.

It lasted almost thirty years.

Starting in 2008, I was forced to rewrite it all.

The Second Draft

At any given moment, there is perhaps no single person who embodies America and what it means to be a real American more than the president.

As a kid, I dreamt about becoming president. To me, it wasn't just about success or service. It was also about winning the Senior Cup at the most extreme level possible. The idea never progressed beyond a daydream. I knew a nonwhite American could never be president. In fact, getting elected at any level as a nonwhite American back then generally required having a majority in your constituency who looked like you. Still, I was drawn to the politics of this country because I saw it as the principal way we wrote and rewrote our national story. And so, early on I decided that if I couldn't become president, I would cover the president as a reporter.

To launch my career, I went overseas with CNN. Within five years, I had become one of CNN's most prominent foreign correspondents, well on my way to becoming a White House correspondent. Along the way, no matter how far I was from home, I never escaped that core struggle about whether I was a real American. As I traveled to dozens of countries, people would always ask, "What are you?," harkening back to my days in Wellesley. "American," I would say, until the awkward silence would compel me to say, "But my parents are from India." "That's it! You are Indian, not American! We love Bollywood!" In ways I didn't fully pick up at the time, the world outside America understood the great caveat to America's promise better than I did.

In 2008, as America was preparing to elect a new president, something fundamental about that great caveat started to change. Democratic primary after Democratic primary, a new figure was emerging as the future of the party and potentially the country. Win by win,

Barack Obama was dismantling my childhood assumption that a nonwhite American could never be president. That was exciting. Beckoning, even.

In mid-May, the beckoning grew deafening. At a rally in Portland, Oregon, Obama stood before seventy-five thousand people. The news clips of that day showed him in the midst of an ocean of supporters. An ocean of hope. I stared at those images obsessively as I sat at my desk in Cairo, Egypt. Seven thousand miles away, I could feel the energy in that crowd and across that campaign. I had spent years abroad at this point, including a year in Baghdad during the worst of the Iraq War. It was that moment in May when America felt the farthest away, because I so deeply wanted to be part of the movement that was building.

A few days later, with one email, I resigned from CNN and gave up everything I had built. I had no promise of a job or even an interview with the Obama campaign. All I had was the belief that I was going to be part of the moment unfolding back home. In so many ways, that move was the riskiest of my life. It was also the easiest. Perhaps the same could be said of my dad's decision to leave everyone and everything he knew behind in India to come to America back in 1961.

When I showed up in Chicago a few weeks later, I started out as an unpaid intern. Friends, family, and peers at CNN thought I was insane. Insane for leaving journalism, insane for joining a campaign that hadn't even won yet, and, most of all, insane for joining the campaign of a man who could never win. Not because he wasn't a good candidate—he was a phenomenal candidate. To them, he couldn't win because he was Black.

I saw it differently. I saw the Obama campaign as a moment of rewrite for America where we would, inevitably, progress forward. Just like we always had before.

In November, Obama won. The world changed. And so did I.

In the Obama administration, I first worked as a speechwriter for the Treasury Secretary before making my way to the White House as the first Indian American speechwriter to a president. All of that made me feel like I was becoming kind of a real American. I was writing about America, helping shape policies in America, helping define the future for America. If the president was the embodiment of a real American, then those working for the president were surely the same.

The moment this realization hit fully was on a Friday night in 2013, when I was drafting a speech for President Obama advocating immigration reform.

The ending of a presidential speech is where a speechwriter tries to land a rallying cry for the nation. For this speech, I anchored the ending around the story of my parents, pulling them from the sidelines of American life and placing them directly into the mainstream of America, not by diminishing their identity as immigrants but, instead, by calling it out:

> There are few things that are more important to us as a society than who gets to come here and call our country home; who gets the privilege of becoming a citizen of the United States of America. That's a big deal.
>
> When we talk about that in the abstract, it's easy sometimes for the discussion to take on a feeling of "us" versus "them." And when that happens, a lot of folks forget that most of "us" used to be "them." . . .
>
> The Irish who left behind a land of famine. The Germans who fled persecution. The Scandinavians who arrived eager to pioneer out west. The Polish. The Russians. The Italians. The

Chinese. The Japanese. The West Indians. The huddled masses who came through Ellis Island on one coast and Angel Island on the other. All those folks, before they were "us," they were "them."

And when each new wave of immigrants arrived, they faced resistance from those who were already here. They faced hardship. They faced racism. They faced ridicule. But over time, as they went about their daily lives, as they earned a living, as they raised a family, as they built a community, as their kids went to school here, they did their part to build a nation.

Build a nation.

When I was a kid, one of the limits I conceded about not being a real American was that I had no ability to question things about America. To challenge things about America. To change things in America. When I was growing up, America was always someone else's, never fully mine.

Imagine, then, what it was like to stand just to the side of the stage while the president of the United States said words that, more than the fact that I had helped craft them, were words I wish a president had said to me when I was a kid. That immigrants and the children of immigrants were as American as anyone else and as able to shape the direction of this country as anyone else.

When he finished, I was beaming uncontrollably, just like I had on the night of my high-school graduation celebrating the Senior Cup and my acceptance into white American culture. This time I was beaming in celebration of my belonging, as a child of immigrants, in America. A belonging bestowed on me by our first Black president.

From that day on, I saw myself as more American than before. And I felt more hopeful about America than ever before. Barack Obama had not just delivered a more equal and just nation during his two terms. He also expanded the definition of a real American to be about more than just white Americans. Irreversibly, I thought.

I was wrong.

The Third Draft

On May 8, 2020, just weeks away from turning forty-one and having spent most of those years trying to become white, I became nonwhite. Not to others, of course—to varying degrees, I had always been nonwhite to others. What made that day unique is that I became a nonwhite American to myself. No more aspiring American. No more aspiring white American. No more immigrant or Indian or South Asian or Asian American. I was a nonwhite American. Married to a nonwhite woman in America. Raising two nonwhite girls in America.

Seismic shifts like that don't happen overnight. They build. This one had been building for three and a half years, with the Trump presidency acting like a powerful wind blowing away a dense fog that had blanketed me for decades until it revealed, ultimately, a truth as clear as day—that systemic racism was alive and well in our time and that by seeking to be the best white version of myself possible, I was complicit in its existence.

The wind started with Trump's Muslim ban, which compelled me, a now proud son of immigrants, to protest at the San Francisco airport with a sign that read, "We are all immigrants," a sentiment I had written into a speech for one president that I was now using to protest another.

The wind grew more forceful when white supremacists protested in Charlottesville and President Trump suggested some of them were "very fine people." It grew more forceful when, in a meeting in the

Oval Office, President Trump talked about Haiti and African countries as "shithole countries." It grew more forceful when, on Twitter,
he said four Members of Congress, all but one of whom were born
in the United States and all of whom are women of color, should "go
back" to where they came from.

Ultimately, the wind grew to be a hurricane when Breonna Tay-
lor and Ahmaud Arbery were killed, each just the latest in what was
starting to feel like an unrelenting string of murders of unarmed Black
Americans.

I had spent so long trying to be white in America, I never stopped
to see what it meant to be Black in America. The Trump years
forced that shift. All these truths I had held to be self-evident about
America—truths that were proven, I thought, by my success as an
Asian American—were not truths at all. They were privileges.

Day by day, as the fog cleared, I started to rethink progress in
America. For decades, I had understood it to be the ability for a
growing number of nonwhite Americans to access the opportunities
afforded to white America. Instead, I was coming to realize that progress should be measured by our ability to increasingly dislodge opportunity in America from the need to assimilate into white America. By
that metric, as Trump's America made clear, we were failing.

That was all swirling in my head the afternoon of May 8, 2020,
when hundreds of former staffers in the Obama administration gathered over Zoom to hear former president Obama make the case for
why we should all get involved with the Biden campaign.

There was something different about hearing Obama talk that
May, certainly compared to May 2008, when he spoke to tens of thousands of mostly white supporters in Portland. The message then was
hope; the message now was survival. The America that we all believed

in, one that was about equality and justice for all, was perilously close to being lost.

Seventeen days later, George Floyd would breathe his last breath on a video that would unleash a global outcry. That moment would make clear that, as a nation, we could never say that we had never been told, or had never seen, the wrenching realities of systemic racism in our past and in our present. If we did nothing about it, I knew we were headed to a dark place.

After logging off the call with President Obama, I sat for a few minutes in silence. Something had changed in me, but I didn't know exactly what. An hour or so later, I took to social media to write a post. In it, I talked about my past as a white-modeling American. I talked about my reverence for the American presidency. And I talked about how President Trump—through his words, his deeds, and the signals he was sending to my girls about America—had shifted me, in fundamental ways, from being white modeling in America to being nonwhite in America. In writing those words, where I was identifying myself as a nonwhite American, I immediately reset my relationship with white America, no longer assuming the baseline for how I should think about myself is how white America thinks about me.

That moment, I also reset my relationship with communities of color in America and, in particular, Black and Native Americans. Those Americans bear the scars, still today, of the original sins of this nation. So many generations of Black and Native Americans have lived and died knowing that at no point in their entire life would their country see them as whole. I can see now that the fact that Black and Native Americans remain so committed to bettering this nation, despite all they have endured, is the real way to define American exceptionalism.

But that awareness wasn't enough. Allyship wasn't enough. As an Asian American, there was something else I had to offer. I had to offer honesty about my role in systemic racism.

As a community, we undeniably face anti-Asian racism. If we choose to see it, we also face the harsh reality that we are often complicit in systemic racism, especially in anti-Black systemic racism. As we lean into our proximity to whiteness, we only support the idea that at the base of being American is being white. I had spent the better part of my life doing just that. Not anymore.

America's story is a messy one rife with contradiction and confusion. But there is one thing that remains constant. Even if we are not always ever-perfecting, we are ever-*evolving*. We are a story in perpetual motion, which means there is always an opportunity to rewrite the story.

At any time you choose, including right now, you can do what I did and rewrite *your* story of self and of country.

That starts with realizing you don't have to be white to be a real American. You don't have to be a fifth-generation American to be a real American. You don't have to have the right name or follow the right faith or live in the right zip code or wear the right clothes or eat the right food to be a real American. None of that matters. The only thing that matters when it comes to whether you are a real American is whether you believe that you are a real American.

When you do, it's a powerful thing. I now feel a deeper level of belonging and a deeper level of confidence—even entitlement—to talk about this country as my own. And just like America, while my story was not always forward moving, it was always moving. Always being rewritten. And today, as a result, this country is no longer an opportunity. It is home.

If enough Asian Americans find our way to feel the same, if enough of us define ourselves not by our proximity to whiteness but by the unique role we can play in unwinding systemic racism from our society, we can be among the most important authors of one of the greatest rewrites in American history. We can make ours the story of a diverse democracy where no one group has a majority but where all groups have equal access to opportunity. We can be the people who make this the place where anyone from anywhere can do anything.

At the beginning, I wasn't American.

Today, I can't think of how I could be any more American.

Museum in Her Head

by Marie Lu

Welcome to the museum in her head
A collection of memories
Ripples on the surface of her life

In the hall to your left
a series of portraits
Here is a little girl whose first American home is New Orleans
whose first American experience is Mardi Gras
Here is a sculpture of fat magnolia leaves
A jar of air heavy with heat and rain
Here is a diorama of her school full of friends
and the bust of a white lady who leaned down to her in concern
asking,
"Honey, aren't there any white children in your school?"

and the little girl answering, confused,
because she didn't yet understand what race meant,
"I'm white"

On the pedestal to your right are a plastic grocery bag and a
    Tupperware
filled with the best homemade Chinese dumplings ever made
Here is a replica of the brown paper bag lunch
and the ham sandwich
that the little girl actually wanted to bring to school
so the other kids would stop laughing at her food
Here is a black-and-white photo of her mother
quietly packing a sandwich for her after she came home and
    complained

In this room is an installation of a closet
a replica of the restaurant closet the little girl spent long days in
waiting for her mother's waitressing shift to end
watching a small TV and dreaming of other worlds
This wall contains a mosaic of her sketches and writing
Early evidence of fantasy stories and dark science fiction worlds
Write what you know is a neon light on this wall
This is what she was taught
so the first worlds she wrote into existence were exactly like the
    books she knew
Filled only with white people

. . .

Upstairs, you will see a wall with frames containing her grade-school
    homework
written with her Chinese name in the top left corner
On the opposite wall, you will see the shift when
she replaces her Chinese name with an English one
because her teachers can never pronounce Xiwei
She-Way
because her classmates called her
She Went That Way
She What
She Weighs a Thousand Pounds
Here is a dictionary flipped open to
her name's real meaning
Hope for the future

On the third floor is a room of glass display cases showing
her likes on the left, dislikes on the right
afternoon tea, flowers, Christmas, video games
                                butternut squash, alcohol, raisins, nightclubs
Down this hall is her preserved teenage bedroom
showcasing posters of Britney Spears and the Backstreet Boys
her old Sega Genesis
a manila folder holding old exams containing grades from As to Ds
a diary about all her crushes
shelves and shelves and shelves of fantasy and science fiction
    paperbacks

This is a floor of all the things about her that have no label of
    Asian
No one ever seems to see this floor

Here are two recordings
comparing how she usually speaks
to how that accent changes
whenever she's in a small southern town
How she exaggerates the accent beyond perfection
extra heavy on the *r*'s
raising the *a*'s
so you know for sure that yes, she is American
She's not a threat
Don't hurt her

Here is a painting with a black silhouette on it
The hole she becomes
when she can't say to her parents how she feels
because they have survived revolutions, seen friends killed, fled
    dictators
crossed oceans with four hundred dollars and nothing else
picked New Orleans so they wouldn't die of cold should they go
    homeless
because their trauma is a trauma she can never understand
so how can she tell them about how some people are mean to her in
    school?

    . . .

On the third floor, you will find
a collection of drafts of her first published novel
along with the inner monologue that haunted her dreams
The same questions over and over
If I write myself into my stories,
Will I only ever be shelved under "Asian American Studies"?
Will I only ever be called an Asian American author?
Will I only ever be allowed to write about my pain?
Will I end my career?
So instead, she sneaks herself into those early stories
Subtle mentions of her heritage and identity
Maybe white readers will mind less if she's barely noticeable

Here is the room where everything changed
Every inch of the walls is filled with letters she has received from her
    readers
They are written by children and teenagers
Readers who are the age she was when she became a reader
They say
I saw myself in your book
I saw you mention a food I love to eat
I saw you insert a tradition I follow
I saw a character who looks like me

This is when she realized
There are others searching for

what she was searching for
Sometimes you can be the one who gives it to them.

The final room is a room of alternate endings
What this museum could have looked like
A diorama where the little girl brings her mother's cooking to
    school
Where she keeps her own name and insists others learn it
Where she doesn't exaggerate her accent
Where she sits down and talks to her parents
Where she writes herself
unapologetically
into her work

This room can be the room of the next little girl.

If you look carefully as you exit
You will notice the blank walls throughout the museum
are not blank at all
There is a sentence written over and over on them
It says

Do not make yourself small
just to appease others
when you can fill up the sky.

It's an honor just to be Asian.

—SANDRA OH

Afterword

Books are sometimes windows, offering views of worlds that may be real or imagined, familiar or strange. These windows are also sliding glass doors, and readers have only to walk through in imagination to become part of whatever world has been created or recreated by the author. When lighting conditions are just right, however, a window can also be a mirror.

—DR. RUDINE SIMS BISHOP,
"Mirrors, Windows, and Sliding Glass Doors"

In April 2021, we had just crossed the one-year mark on the COVID-19-induced lockdown, our country was reeling from the recent Atlanta spa shootings where six Asian women were murdered, and Asians in America were facing yet another major spike in anti-Asian hate. In fact, between March 2020 and April 2021 over 6,600 hate incidents against Asians in America were reported to Stop AAPI Hate. And in April 2021 the violence had reached a fever pitch that had finally broken through to mainstream media. It was a cruel month. It is against this backdrop that this book was born. Out of hate, love. In isolation, connection.

As with most things in my lockdown life at the time, it started with an email. Christian Trimmer, the publisher of MTV Books, reached out for guidance. He had an idea for a book about growing up Asian in America. His vision was a compilation of essays and stories that reflected the vast experiences of being Asian American and was, in short, a book he wished he had been able to read as a young adult. We immediately fell in love with both the concept and Christian. The partnership was electric, and we were abuzz with ideas and suggestions. Could we get SuChin Pak (SuChin Pak!) to do the introduction? Alongside ethnicity, gender identity, and generation, could we also consider age and geographic diversity? Could we get thirty entries for CAPE's thirtieth anniversary of fighting for Asian American and Pacific Islander representation in Hollywood?

The volley of thoughts and potential contributors led to an ever-growing spreadsheet (*naturally*), and our excitement escalated as each contributor confirmed their participation. On the CAPE side, our communications manager, Jes Vu, shepherded this project and led our team in brainstorming potential contributors. In collaboration with Christian's curation and outreach, the collection swiftly crystallized with formats as varied as their content: essays, poems, comics panels, and even a one-act monologue play. Thirty gifted storytellers contributed pieces in their individual voices and styles, resulting in this special book.

To be Asian in America is a multifaceted, intersectional, and varied experience. As underscored by the variety of stories and viewpoints contained in these pages, we are not a monolith; we are an umbrella.

Moreover, as these stories illuminate, identity is an evolving and ever-changing journey of self-discovery.

Reading these reflections is like being invited into someone's soul. Their memories and defining moments. Their hopes and aspirations. Pain. Discovery. Loss. Anger. Growth. Joy. Myriad emotions swirling and colliding through a journey of lives lived and shared through these pages. Different but similar. We are Asian. We are American.

SuChin's introduction discusses *han* and the different types of courage reflected in this book. Indeed, many stories recount painful memories, private thoughts, and personal revelations requiring great vulnerability and courage to share. The Moth trains us to tell stories about scars, not wounds, and the pieces in this book deftly thread that needle. In some instances, these are not easy stories to share, and we are grateful to the authors for allowing us to include them in this book.

Many contributors discussed feeling the need to hide their light and make themselves small. There was a common thread of the desire to blend in so as not to elicit undue negative attention. Time and again, this is a common refrain in our communities. My hope is that readers who feel the same way will be comforted in knowing they are not alone and perhaps even be disabused of this feeling. It's all right (nay, encouraged) to toot your own horn and accept credit where credit is due.

There are also the triumphant stories of righteous anger, pride, and allyship. Many expressed their journey from shame to pride in their Asian heritage. Some acknowledged their privilege and adjacency to whiteness as we collectively band together against white supremacy to build a more equitable world.

The stories contained in this book are a snapshot in time, as well as a benchmark against which future generations can measure our collective progress.

I laughed. I cried. I cheered. My heart feels bigger somehow. Fuller. More interconnected. I felt seen in ways I wasn't expecting, and I gained new perspectives. In many ways, I think that's the purpose of this book. It's a safe haven of windows, mirrors, and sliding glass doors where we can collectively heal through sharing our scars. This is what community feels like.

For anyone who has felt othered, misunderstood, or insignificant, this book is for you. For anyone who has learned (or is still learning) to embrace, celebrate, and share unapologetically who you are, this book is for you. Whether you are of Asian descent and born in America or immigrated later, this book is for you.

I was late to the Asian American party, but once I arrived, fighting for representation became a lifelong mission for me.

Growing up as a fourth-generation Japanese American in Honolulu, Hawaii, I was blissfully ignorant of the plight of Asians in the rest of America until I arrived in beautiful but smoggy Los Angeles, California, for college. A native English speaker, I suddenly had to learn some new vocabulary, like "trash" instead of "rubbish" and "Asian" instead of "Oriental"—yes, I was still saying "Oriental," as there was no negative connotation with the term in Hawaii at the time.

Unaware that the path I was embarking on would shape the rest of my life, I enrolled in my first Asian American Studies class my freshman year. This book would have been the perfect complement to the historical textbooks we studied, and I would have loved to have read it back then. Outside of class, I was also learning a lot from my classmates and their experiences growing up Asian in America. I learned about history and intergenerational trauma, which led to that cute Korean guy's parents refusing to let him date a Japanese girl like me. I learned the vernacular and confidence to speak cogently about the issues affecting our communities, which I further honed during my internship at OCA-Asian Pacific American Advocates in Washington, DC, during my junior year. It was my first experience working in the nonprofit, civil rights space, and I was able to work on national issues affecting Asian Americans. Then in my senior year, I ultimately minored in Asian American Studies and was part of a small group of students who were finally able to finish a decades-long struggle to establish an Asian American Studies Department, including a full-fledged major (which started after I graduated). I've since become an adjunct professor for the department, and many stories from my students mirror the sentiments found in this book. Change is always slower than we wish it to be.

In my first career as an attorney, through advocacy organizations such as the Asian Pacific American Bar Association of Los Angeles County and the Multicultural Bar Alliance of Southern California, we fought for civil rights and representation on the bench and in academia, among other things. We celebrated successes and pushed for more. In my current role at CAPE, I continue to fight for representation in a different realm—media. While there have been great strides made since I started in 2015, we still have a long way to go. Sometimes it astounds me that there are still so many "firsts" to celebrate. For example, the 2021 Academy Awards saw many historic moments, including Yuh-Jung Youn being the first South Korean woman to win Best Actress in a Supporting Role, Steven Yeun being the first Asian American man to be nominated for Best Actor in a Leading Role, Riz Ahmed being the first Muslim performer nominated for Best Actor in a Leading Role, and Chloé Zhao being the first woman of color to win for Best Director.

This is why representation and books like this matter.

At CAPE, we work to shift culture through storytelling to create a better world. What we watch on our screens should reflect the world in which we live and project a better one. CAPE has actively supported writers for over two decades, because we know representation starts on the page. Authentic stories of lived experiences, such as those found in this book, are an important and powerful way to foster understanding and acceptance.

Stories matter because they affect our perceptions of others, as well as of ourselves. The stories we tell ourselves shape who we are and what we can become. They can affect the size of our dreams and even circumscribe our potential. What stories are you telling yourself? Do they serve you? Is it time to let them go?

This book—for us, by us—is an important addition to the contemporary nonfiction landscape. A veritable compendium of layered and nuanced reflections, these stories provide the antidote to the damaging stereotypes long peddled by Hollywood and consumed by everyone from Main Street to Wall Street. Asians in America face stereotypes of being quiet, submissive, nerdy, exotic, and foreign, among others. Real-life stories from Asian Americans from all walks of life such as those contained in this book combat such limited, one-dimensional portrayals and highlight our humanity. These stories portray the breadth and depth of what it means to be Asian in America.

I was late to the Asian American party, and now there's no place I'd rather be.

Michelle K. Sugihara, CAPE Executive Director
September 2021

Acknowledgments

Special thanks to:

Xavier Afriyie	Abe Chang
Noopur Agarwal	John Cheng
the AMP Leadership Team	Sarah DeFilippis
Amal Baggar	Nina Diaz
Daylee Baker	Lauren Epstein
Thomas Berger	Jo Flattery
Jennifer Besser	Meredith Goldberg-Morse
Ruhi Bhalla	Meghan Hooper
James Blue	Melanie Iglesias
Gregory Bonsignore	Heather Johns
Pamela Brill	Jess Ju
Liz Byer	Falon Kirby
Nihal Catkal	Laywan Kwan

Sharon Kwon

Carina Licon

India Little

Lourdes Lopez

Andrew Lutin

Paige Lytle

Chris McCarthy

Libby McGuire

Rhian Moore

Eve Nguyen

Raaga Rajagopala

Eric Reyes

Justin Rosenblatt

Lance Rusoff

Leshelle Sargent

Dana Sloan

Rachel Thanasoulis

Martha Tobar

Rachel Tung

Jes Vu

Jessica Zalkind

Resources

CAPE USA, https://www.capeusa.org/

Asian Americans Advancing Justice,
 https://www.advancingjustice-aajc.org/

Asian Health Services, https://asianhealthservices.org/

Asian Mental Health Collective, https://www.asianmhc.org/

Asians Speak Up, https://asiansspeakup.org/

Crisis Text Line, https://www.crisistextline.org/

National Alliance on Mental Health Illness, https://nami.org/

National Asian American Pacific Islander Mental Health
 Association, https://www.naapimha.org/

New Breath Foundation, https://new-breath.org/

Stop AAPI Hate, https://stopaapihate.org/

The Trevor Project, https://www.thetrevorproject.org/

Quotation Sources

9   *Patiently educating a clueless white person:* Cathy Park Hong, *Minor Feelings: An Asian American Reckoning,* (New York: One World, 2020).

47   *When people see us as heroes:* Jeff Yang, "Asian Americans Are Finally Getting the Heroes We Deserve," *New York Times,* September 2, 2021.

77   *My dad's from that generation:* Hasan Minhaj, "Comic Hasan Minhaj on Roasting Trump and Growing Up a 'Third Culture Kid,'" interview by David Bianculli, *Fresh Air,* NPR, May 18, 2017.

105   *I only care if my mom is proud:* Bretman Rock (@bretmanrock), "I only care if my mom is proud of me," Twitter, July 18, 2021, 12:51 a.m.

137   *There is value in choosing:* Celeste Ng, "Keeping Love Close," *New York Times,* April 8, 2021.

167   *[It] is a part of the bitter undercurrent:* Wesley Yang, "Paper Tigers," *New York,* May 6, 2011.

189 *When I'm here in America:* Steven Yeun, quoted in, Jay Caspian Kang, "The Many Lives of Steven Yeun," *New York Times Magazine*, February 3, 2021.

225 *It's an honor just:* Sandra Oh, in "70th Emmy Awards: We Solved It!" Television Academy, posted September 17, 2018, YouTube video, 1:31, https://www.youtube.com/watch?v= J74hHQgCjrc.

Biographies

CAPE (Coalition of Asian Pacifics in Entertainment) is the premier nonprofit organization creating opportunities and driving Asian and Pacific Islander (API) success in Hollywood. It works to shift culture through storytelling to establish a better world. Since 1991, CAPE has fought for API representation in film and television through (1) nurturing and engaging creative talent and executive leadership; (2) providing cultural content consulting and talent referrals; and (3) championing projects for critical box office and streaming success. A mighty force in Hollywood, CAPE creates community for emerging and established API professionals behind and in front of the camera, and has helped improve the landscape, relevance, and power of APIs in the entertainment industry. Learn more at capeusa.org and @capeusa on IG/Twitter.

SuChin Pak is a veteran journalist who has been hosting and reporting the news for over twenty-five years. She has reported on ABC, NBC, Discovery Networks, Oxygen, and E! She is most known for her long tenure as the first Asian American reporter for MTV News. From hosting red-carpet shows to reporting on presidential elections and international relief efforts to covering some of the biggest headlines in news, Pak has been a dedicated journalist since reporting on her first show at the age of sixteen. She currently cohosts a podcast, *Add to Cart*, about consumerism and what it says about who we are. She has focused much of her work on issues involving social change.

Heather Jeng Bladt is a screenwriter whose credits include the Netflix series *Orange Is the New Black* and *Social Distance* and AMC's *Mad Men*. She is a third-generation Chinese American and a SoCal girl, born and bred. She grew up in Orange County and attended the University of Southern California's School of Cinema-Television, where she earned her BFA in writing for screen and television. She lives in Los Angeles and can often be found eating Baskin-Robbins with her husband, Christian, and two children, Felix and Lucy.

Melissa de la Cruz is the best-selling author of numerous critically acclaimed and award-winning novels. Many of her more than fifty books have topped the *New York Times*, *USA Today*, and *Los Angeles Times* best-seller lists and have been published in over twenty countries. Notable titles include the books in the Descendants, Blue Bloods, Witches of East End, and Alex & Eliza series. De la Cruz also developed the films *Christmas in Angel Falls* and *Pride, Prejudice and Mistletoe* (based on her novel) for the Hallmark Channel. She lives in West Hollywood, California, with her husband and daughter. Visit melissa-delacruz.com.

H'Rina DeTroy teaches private essays, editing, and cultivating creativity. She was the recipient of the Cafe Royal Cultural Foundations Winter 2020 Grant in Literature and the 2019 Emerging Writer Fellowship at Aspen Word in Memoir. Her personal essay "Knot" was published in the anthology *Borderlands and Crossroads: Writing the Motherland*. She created Apocalypse Never: Writing Our Origin Stories and Imaginative Futures as Montagnard Americans, a writing workshop that centers the Montagnard American and diasporic experience. She has master's degrees in journalism and creative writing.

Dương Nguyễn Ca Dao, or Cookie, was born in Vietnam and grew up in the United States. She graduated from the University of Southern California with a bachelor's in international relations and global business. She is the cofounder of Người Thông Dịch, or The Interpreter, alongside USC fellow Jady Chan, which aims to build a bridge between elder communities and younger generations of Vietnamese Americans and to empower Vietnamese people across the diaspora to participate in the political process of their adopted countries. Cookie currently works as a risk consultant for a Fortune 500 firm.

Gayle Gaviola is a publicist, culinary-school dropout, and Filipina American military brat with no set "hometown." She currently leads communications and publicity for ViacomCBS's Gen Z scripted and digital studio, Awesomeness, and cochairs ViacomCBS's AAPI employee resource group, AMP. A graduate of the University of California at Santa Barbara, she now resides in Los Angeles. In her spare time, she loves to snowboard and write. She is working on her first novel.

Teresa Hsiao is the cocreator, writer, and executive producer of *Awkwafina Is Nora from Queens* on Comedy Central. Teresa started her career in animation, writing on shows such as *American Dad* and *Family Guy*. She has developed TV pilots for Sony, 20th Century Fox, and Warner Horizon, and currently has a feature in development at Lionsgate. Originally from Boston, Teresa graduated from Harvard with a degree in economics. She currently resides in Los Angeles.

Shing Yin Khor is a cartoonist and installation artist exploring the Americana mythos and new human rituals. A Malaysian-Chinese immigrant, and an American citizen since 2011, they are the author of *The Legend of Auntie Po*, a historical fiction graphic novel about Chinese labor in 1800s logging camps and Paul Bunyan stories, and *The American Dream?*, a graphic novel memoir about traveling Route 66.

Yoonj Kim is an award-winning journalist and producer who has received recognition for her coverage of environmental and indigenous rights, drug trafficking, and the 2020 presidential race. She's currently the Social Impact Correspondent at MTV News. Prior to that, she hosted documentaries for Playboy, Mic, and Pivot TV. Her op-eds on politics, inequality, and Asian American issues have been published in the *Guardian*, the *Washington Post*, the *Los Angeles Times*, and more, and she's spoken on the same topics on MSNBC, *Entertainment*

Tonight, and other television outlets. She is a graduate of Northwestern University.

———

Mark Kramer is a comedy writer living in LA after spending his entire life in New York. He grew up the son of a Filipina immigrant and a Jewish Brooklyn Dodgers fan, on Staten Island—where "diversity" meant serving tomato sauce *and* alfredo. Before becoming a professional writer, he took many formative detours, like working at a juice bar for meatheads, making websites for a Mafia-connected Scientologist, passing all four parts of the C.P.A. exam, and sadly more. Mark is currently an Emmy Award–winning staff writer for *Last Week Tonight with John Oliver*.

———

David Kwong delights and challenges audiences around the world with his intellectual brand of magic. A veteran "cruciverbalist" (crossword puzzle constructor), Kwong routinely creates puzzles for the *New York Times*, *Los Angeles Times*, and *Wall Street Journal*. His one-man show, *The Enigmatist*, played 125 sold-out performances in New York before premiering in Los Angeles in 2021. He is also the creator of the virtual show *Inside the Box* and the author of *Spellbound: Seven Principles of Illusion to Captivate Audiences and Unlock the Secrets of Success*. Kwong is a graduate of Harvard University. Learn more at davidkwongmagic.com.

———

Edmund Lee covers the media industry for the *New York Times*. He has chronicled the radical changes upending the news and entertainment industries. Prior to that, he was the managing editor at Vox Media's Recode, where he oversaw a group of editors and reporters since 2014. He has also written for *Bloomberg Businessweek*, *Advertising Age*, *Portfolio* magazine, and *Women's Wear Daily*. He started his career at the *Village Voice*. He has also worked as a screenwriter, and in 2007 his original film, *West 32nd*, premiered at the Tribeca Film Festival. Mr. Lee lives in Brooklyn with his family.

Marie Lu is the #1 *New York Times* best-selling author of multiple books, among them *Legend*, *The Young Elites*, *Warcross*, and *Skyhunter*. She graduated from the University of Southern California and jumped into the video game industry, where she worked as an artist. A full-time writer, she spends her spare hours reading, drawing, playing games, and getting stuck in traffic. She lives in the traffic-jam capital, Los Angeles, with her illustrator/author husband, Primo Gallanosa, and their son.

Kimiko Matsuda-Lawrence is a writer-director hailing from Washington, DC, and Honolulu, Hawaii. Raised in a family of critical race theorists and freedom fighters, she has always been drawn to storytelling as a means to building a new world. After working in theater in New York, Kimiko transitioned to television and film, writing for the TV shows *Twenties* and *Boomerang*. Her past work includes the plays *Holding: A Queer Black Love Story*; *Black Magic*; and *I, Too, Am Harvard* (also a viral photo campaign). More recently, she produced the short film *little trumpet*. Visit kimikomatsudalawrence.com.

Michelle Myers is an award-winning poet and educator. Appearing on HBO's *Def Poetry Jam* as a founding member of Yellow Rage, Michelle harnesses her experiences as a biracial Korean American woman to create work that raises awareness and builds community. Her writing has been published in *Apiary*, the *Philadelphia Inquirer*, *Title Magazine*, *Brevity*, and *USA Today*. Her poetry also has received recognition from the Leeway Foundation, Loft Literary Center, Asian Arts Initiative, and Dodge Poetry Program. Michelle currently serves on the Advisory Board of the Berrie Center, and her CCPTV show *Drop the Mic* has been nominated for six Emmys.

Amna Nawaz is an Emmy and Peabody award–winning journalist, serving as the Chief Correspondent and Primary Substitute Anchor for the *PBS NewsHour*. Prior to joining the *NewsHour* Nawaz was an anchor and correspondent at ABC News, and before that she served as a foreign correspondent at NBC News. She is also the founding editor of *NBC Asian America*. Nawaz is the first Asian American and Muslim American in history to moderate a US presidential debate. She is a graduate of the University of Pennsylvania and the London School of Economics. She lives with her husband and two daughters in the Washington, DC, area.

Riss M. Neilson is the author of the young-adult novel *Deep in Providence*. A Magna Cum Laude graduate of Rhode Island College, she won the English department's Jean Garrigue Award, which was judged by novelist Nick White. She is from Providence, Rhode Island, and lives for the city's art and culture scene. When she's not writing, she's watching anime or playing video games with her two children.

Trung Le Nguyen, also known as Trungles, is a Vietnamese American comic book artist and storyteller from Minnesota. He was born in a refugee camp somewhere in the Philippine province of Palawan. Trung has contributed work for Oni Press, Boom! Studios, and Image Comics, largely in the romance genre. His first original graphic novel, *The Magic Fish*, was published in 2020 through Random House Graphic. He currently lives in Minneapolis, Minnesota, and is raising three very spoiled hens.

Ellen K. Pao is a tech investor and advocate, the former CEO of Reddit, and a cofounder and CEO of the award-winning diversity and inclusion nonprofit Project Include. Her writing has appeared in WIRED, the *New York Times*, the *Washington Post*, *Time*, Lenny, and Recode. She has earned an electrical engineering degree from Princeton and law and business degrees from Harvard. Visit ellenkpao.com.

Moss Perricone is a Brooklyn-based writer. He wrote for Netflix's *Patriot Act with Hasan Minhaj*, where he won a Peabody Award. He also wrote for *The Other Two* and the reboot of *Beavis and Butt-Head*. His fiction has appeared in the *Southern Indiana Review*.

Aneesh Raman has spent the past two decades working everywhere from war zones to the White House, from early-stage start-ups to global enterprises. He currently leads strategic communications at LinkedIn. Previously, he was a Senior Economic Advisor for California governor Gavin Newsom and Head of Economic Impact at Facebook. From 2009 to 2013, he worked for the Obama administration, including as a speechwriter to President Barack Obama. Raman started his career as a CNN war correspondent. A Harvard graduate, he is a former Fulbright scholar and term member at the Council on Foreign Relations and is a member of the John F. Kennedy Presidential Library New Frontier Committee.

Nathan Ramos-Park is an award-winning writer, actor, and musician from the Midwest. He has written television/film for Netflix, Disney, Nickelodeon, Amazon, and more. Previously, he was a songwriter and creative producer for *Club Mickey Mouse*. His play, *As We Babble On*, had a lauded world premiere at East West Players in 2018. And his song "Gay Asian Country Love Song" was a Queerty nominee. Learn more at koreapino.com.

Michelle K. Sugihara is the Executive Director of CAPE (Coalition of Asian Pacifics in Entertainment). She is also an entertainment attorney, film producer, and adjunct professor for the Claremont Colleges' Intercollegiate Department of Asian American Studies. She co-leads #GoldOpen, is on the leadership team of Time's Up Entertainment Women of Color, and is a founding member of the Asian Pacific American Friends of the Theater. She is also an associate member of Cold Tofu, the nation's premier Asian American comedy improv and sketch group. An avid public speaker, Michelle speaks and teaches across the country.

Aisha Sultan is a nationally syndicated columnist and award-winning filmmaker and features writer. Her work has run in more than a hundred publications. She has won several national honors, including the Asian American Journalists Association Excellence in Written Journalism award for her coverage of the unrest in Ferguson, Missouri. Her work explores social change with an emphasis on education, families, and inequality. She teaches college writing at Washington University and speaks at conferences, universities, and training events.

Sokunthary Svay is a Khmer writer from New York City and a founding member of the Cambodian American Literary Arts Association (CALAA). She is the author of *Apsara in New York* and has had her writing anthologized and performed by actors and singers. Svay's first opera, *Woman of Letters*, set by composer Liliya Ugay, received its world premiere at the Kennedy Center in January 2020. She was the recipient of the 2021 OPERA America IDEA Grant for her next opera, *Chhlong Tonle*. She teaches English at Queens College (CUNY).

Tanaïs (née Tanwi Nandini Islam) is the New York–based author of the critically acclaimed novel *Bright Lines*, which was a finalist for the Center for Fiction First Novel Prize, Edmund White Award for Debut Fiction, and Brooklyn Eagles Literary Prize, as well as the essay collection *In Sensorium: Notes for My People*. Over the course of their career, they've worked as a community organizer, a domestic violence court advocate, a probations intake officer, and a youth arts educator. Tanaïs is also a perfumer and the founder of the beauty, fragrance, and design studio TANAÏS. Visit studiotanais.com.

Kim Tran is a writer and consultant who brings social justice lessons to movement, research, and organizational spaces. Her work has been featured in NPR, *Slate*, and the *New York Times*. She is working on a book manuscript about solidarity during Black Lives Matter titled *The End of Allyship: A New Era of Solidarity*.

Catzie Vilayphonh is an award-winning writer, spoken word poet, and multimedia artist, as well as one of the founding members of Yellow Rage. Through her work, she provides an awareness not often heard, drawing from personal narrative. She runs a community arts org, Laos In The House, and is also a commissioner on the Mayor's Commission on Asian American Affairs of Philadelphia and the only noncitizen council member on the Pennsylvania Council on the Arts. A child of refugees, Catzie was born in a camp on the way to America, and thus considers herself part of the ".5 Generation."

G Yamazawa is a Japanese American poet and recording artist born and raised in Durham, North Carolina. A National Poetry Slam

Champion and Kundiman Fellow, G has toured over two hundred universities and is currently working on his fourth full-length studio album.

Kao Kalia Yang is the author of the memoirs *The Latehomecomer: A Hmong Family Memoir, The Song Poet: A Memoir of My Father*, and *Somewhere in the Unknown World: A Collective Refugee Memoir*, as well as the children's books *A Map into the World, The Shared Room, The Most Beautiful Thing*, and *Yang Warriors*. She coedited (with Shannon Gibney) the groundbreaking collection *What God Is Honored Here?: Writings on Miscarriage and Infant Loss by and for Native Women and Women of Color*. Her work has been recognized by the National Endowment for the Arts, the National Book Critics Circle Award, and the PEN Center USA Literary Awards, among others. She lives in Minnesota with her family.